# HAWAI'I Cooks

# A Japanese KITCHEN

## Star★Advertiser

# A Japanese KITCHEN

## Traditional Recipes with an Island Twist

**MURIEL MIURA**

Introduction by
**Arnold Hiura**

Photography by
**Kaz Tanabe**

Illustrations by
**Paul Konishi**

Mutual
Publishing

## DEDICATED TO:

Daughter, Shari Akemi Miura Ling, M.D.
Son-in-law, Geoffrey Ling, M.D., Ph.D., F.A.A.N.
Grandchildren Alissa Sachi & Stephen Minoru Ling

Library of Congress Control Number: 2017946416

ISBN: 978-1939487-83-4

Food photography by Kaz Tanabe (unless otherwise noted)
Illustrations by Paul Konishi
Art direction by Jane Gillespie
Cover design by Jane Gillespie
Design by Courtney Tomasu

First Printing, October 2017

Mutual Publishing, LLC
1215 Center Street, Suite 210
Honolulu, Hawai'i 96816
Ph: 808-732-1709
Fax: 808-734-4094
info@mutualpublishing.com
www.mutualpublishing.com

Printed in South Korea

Photos on pages xxv and 214 are used by permission of the *Honolulu Star-Adveriser*.

Cover image © itonggg | shutterstock
Photos from Dreamstime.com:
pg. i © Phurinee, pg. v © Zoom-zoom, pg. vii © Eedology, pg. xxi © Pontuse, pg. 3 © Korzeniewski, pg. 8 © Hlphoto, pg. 10 © Viva3003, pg. 13 © Alkir, pg. 20 © Omgeijutsuka, pg. 25 © Artcookstudio, pg. 28 © Andrey Starostin, pg. 30 © Paulbrighton, pg. 33, 36, 125, 132, 191 © Ppy2010ha, pg. 35 © Minadezhda, pg. 37 © Reika7, pg. 38 © Haotian, pg. 40 © Youichi, pg. 54 © Akiyoko74, pg. 61 © Contrail1, pg. 66 © Billyphoto2008, pg. 68 © Mexrix, pg. 70 (top) © Ezumeimages, pg. 70 (bottom) © HandmadePictures, pg. 83 © Akiyoko74, pg. 84 © Photos7384, pg. 85 (paper) © Vlntn, pg. 88 © Kitigan, pg. 92 © Creativesunday, pg. 97 © Barol16, pg. 99 © Sutsaiy, pg. 105 © Huzaimewahid, pg. 106, 107 © Looby, pg. 110 © Runinex, pg. 116 © Alexmakarova, pg. 120 © Lightzoom, pg. 124 © Kgtoh`v, pg. 127 © Timmary, pg. 134 © Jedimaster, pg. 135 © Kewuwu, pg. 141 © Macrovector, pg. 143 © Naito8, pg. 147 © Junial, pg. 161 © Kyogo7002, pg. 165 © Msymons, pg. 180 © Torsakarin, pg. 184 © Dimabelokoni, pg. 185 © Bagwold, pg. 187 © Photoankrum, pg. 188 © Peefay, pg. 194 © Advan1240, pg. 198 © Annapustynnikova, pg. 199 © Ballllad, pg. 201 © Yosimasa, pg. 210 (bottom) © Tatulaju, pg. 211 © Akiyoko74, pg. 212 (top) © Jiampp, pg. 213 © Kedsirin; pg. 222 (bamboo shoots) © Toa555, (chestnuts) © Tadeusz Wejkszo, (Chinese cabbage) © Felinda, (eggplant) © Sriharun; pg. 223 (ginger) © Maceofoto, (kampyo) © Gb3621, (cucumber) © Jojojojo, (mizuna) © Tatsuya Otsuka, (lotus root) © Shariff Che\' Lah, (mugwort) © Sommail; pg. 224 (shiitake) © Prapann, (enoki) © Kaiskynet, (shiso) © Pipa100; pg. 225 (daikon) © Sommai Sommai, (wakame) © Harutora, (konbu) © Riverlim; pg. 226 (shoyu) © Ostancov Vladislav, (miso) © Travelling-light; pg. 227 (rice vinegar) © Kellyreekolibry, (mirin) © Kewuwu

# Star ★ Advertiser

I n 2013 the *Honolulu Star-Advertiser* began a partnership with Mutual Publishing in a unique exploration of the many cuisines that make up what we call the island plate. The first cookbook was *A Korean Kitchen,* followed by editions on Portuguese, Okinawan, Chinese and Filipino cuisines. *A Japanese Kitchen* is the sixth in this series.

Although these books are all rooted in tradition, our focus has been on recipes that reflect the way each cuisine has evolved in our islands, to accommodate local ingredients and to suit the tastes of a diverse population.

The writers are from different backgrounds but all grew up with a love of food and a curiosity about cooking. They learned from grandparents, parents, aunties, uncles and an extended network of calabash relatives. Family connections are key.

At the *Honolulu Star-Advertiser* we cover both the roots and the most contemporary expressions of island cuisine on our food pages every week. We proudly build on that purpose with the "Hawai'i Cooks" series.

**Dennis Francis**
President and Publisher,
*Honolulu Star-Advertiser*
and O'ahu Publications

# Contents

## Bento & Zensai
## Box Lunches & Appetizers

## Dashi & Owanrui
## Soup Stocks & Soups

## Gohanmono
## Rice Dishes

## Sushi
## Vinegar-Flavored Rice

## Menrui
## Noodle Dishes

## Aemono, Sunomono, and Tsukemono
## Mixed Foods, Vinegared Salads, and Pickled Vegetables

## Sashimi
### Raw Fish

## Nimono
### Simmered Foods

## Mushimono
### Steamed Foods

## Agemono
### Fried Foods

## Nabemono
## One-Pot Cooking

## Yakimono
## Grilled & Broiled Foods

## Tofu Ryori
## Tofu Dishes

## Okashi
## Desserts & Confectionery

## Nomimono
## Beverages

## Mukimono
## Garnishes

## Traditions and Celebrations

## The Japanese Pantry

## Appendix

# Acknowledgments

Many thanks to my loving family who shared the treasured recipes and tips that inspired me to work on this special publication of *Hawai'i Cooks: A Japanese Kitchen.*

Much love and thanks to my daughter, **Shari Miura Ling, M.D.,** who encouraged me in countless ways during the book's creation and is always my inspiration and best food critic.

Heartfelt thanks to **Jane Gillespie** and **Courtney Tomasu** of Mutual Publishing's production team, who skillfully brought this collection of treasured family recipes, drawings, photos, and memories to life. Their hard work and dedication are reflected throughout the book on every page!

Special thanks to:

**Arnold Hiura**, author and food historian—for sharing his considerable food history and knowledge.

**Betty Shimabukuro**, *Honolulu Star-Advertiser* managing editor—for editing and writing some of the text.

**Paul Konishi**, artist, retired art teacher—for the illustrations and for his friendship, and that of his wife, Arline.

**Lue Zimmelman** of Nuimono—for sharing special Japanese designs for this book, and most of all, for her very special friendship.

**Bennett Hymer**, publisher—for his friendship, faith, and confidence in me.

**Gay Wong**—for her friendship, support, and marketing efforts.

And to my husband, **Yoshio Kaminaka,** who was most patient and supportive during my long hours spent at the computer. Thank you so very much for always joining me on my journeys!

**Muriel Miura**

# The Hawai'i Cooks Series

**M**uriel Miura has been my lunch buddy for nearly two decades. We've planned eight cookbooks during long lunch meetings, starting with *What Hawai'i Likes to Eat*, and continuing through *Hawai'i's Holiday Cookbook* and all the entries in the "Hawai'i Cooks" series.

Through these meal-time meet-ups I've learned a lot about Muriel's background—beginning with her early days as a home economist with the Gas Company, teaching others to cook. In the 1960s she led "Wiki-Wiki Kau Kau" classes at lunchtime. This evolved into one of the original local cooking shows, "Cook Japanese," which Muriel hosted in the early '70s. And that evolved into *Cook Japanese: Hawaiian Style* in 1974, a cookbook classic.

Muriel has told me repeatedly that her aim has always been to capture the traditional Japanese recipes of her family for her grandchildren. She wanted to put on the record the cooking techniques she'd learned from her parents—and the basic home-style recipes that were already being lost by her own generation.

That is the soul of the "Hawai'i Cooks" series, to explore the melting pot of local cooking, culture by culture. In this book we turn to Japanese cuisine, as it has evolved in our islands.

Common sense and an it-better-be-good sense of quality were the trademarks of Muriel's career as a cooking teacher, and she brings both to this book. Let her teach you.

**Betty Shimabukuro**
*Editor*

# Preface
## A FAMILY LEGACY

As I was making rolled sushi recently, I realized how immensely satisfying I found the process. From mincing, chopping, and slicing the vegetables, to cooking them individually to perfection in a shoyu-base sauce, the sights, sounds, and smells were intoxicating. Cooking has, for me at least, never been purely about the result, but the hands-on craft along the way. It's the small details that make it so pleasurable. I'm sure many of you feel the same way.

Preparing food is often described as an art. Nowhere is this description more apt than with Japanese cuisine. The foods of Japan are deliberately prepared to be as beautiful as they are delicious. Japanese dishes, characterized by simplicity, delicacy, and variety, preserve the natural flavor of each ingredient—the true esthetic value of the cuisine.

To know more about the art of Japanese cooking is to learn about the people themselves and their tradition-steeped lore. Their way with food—neat, simple, artistic—is repeated elsewhere in the culture, perhaps best illustrated by the art of Ikebana (flower arrangement).

Well-prepared Japanese food always begins with the freshest possible ingredients, a standard that goes hand-in-hand with the principle of simplicity. Ingredients are prepared with restraint, emphasizing the natural flavors. The goal is to enhance, not mask, qualities of the ingredients. While basic flavors are augmented by sauces and condiments, they never lose their identities.

Elegant simplicity also guides presentation, as small portions of a few foods are gracefully arranged on beautiful dishes in a carefully chosen composition of shapes and colors. The primary appeal is to the senses of sight, scent, and taste. Flavors and fragrances are delicate and often subtly complex. The cuisine is built upon a few

basic items—rice, green tea, seafood, noodles, shoyu, and a colorful variety of vegetables.

Throughout the centuries, Japan has been an eager recipient of influences from overseas. Foreign customs were not always adopted accurately, but always enthusiastically. Japan has imported many culinary traditions since times of antiquity, so a "pure" Japanese style in food preparation is a chimera and always has been.

Only in recent years has the centuries-old culinary art of Japan been enjoyed globally. It has given the Western world a fresh look at familiar ingredients and introduced many healthful and delicious new ones. Traditional Japanese foods, such as tofu, seaweed, and low-sodium miso could easily replace high-cholesterol and high-sodium foods in the Western diet. We might also supplement our diets with more fresh fruits and vegetables, Japanese-style.

My parents taught me that Japanese cooking is not only enjoyable, but economical and time-saving as well. Good Japanese cooking requires a spirit of adventure, an artistic eye, and imagination. It does not require a strict adherence to traditional ingredients, but rather an adaptation of Japanese ideas of arrangement, colors, textures, shapes, and distinctive flavors.

This collection is based upon my Japanese heritage and family traditions, with recipes updated and adapted with an awareness of changing trends and tastes. The dishes also reflect the legacy of the Japanese in Hawai'i. While the simple elegance of Japanese cuisine sets it apart from Hawai'i's other ethnic foods, elements definitely have been borrowed from the island melting pot, and you'll find those adaptations here.

I began sharing my family recipes with *Cook Japanese Hawaiian Style*, published in 1974. *A Japanese Kitchen* over 40 years later completes the task. The book is designed for anyone who loves to cook. While thousands of Japanese recipes are available, *A Japanese Kitchen* is based upon a compilation of my favorite family treasures.

Through the pages of this book, you're invited to explore the fascinating essence of the cuisine, from Zensai (appetizers) to Okashi (desserts). *A Japanese Kitchen* is designed for all cooks to have fun with Japanese cooking.

The mystique surrounding the preparation and cooking of exotic Japanese foods is dispelled by simple directions and each recipe has been kitchen-tested and developed to meet today's palates, but individual tastes differ. Please use the recipes only as a guide as you develop your variations, your own family traditions.

*A Japanese Kitchen* represents the contributions of many. It is published with today's generation in mind, with the hope of contributing to a deeper appreciation of Hawai'i-style Japanese cooking, and of preserving that legacy for the next generation. My heart-

*Celebrating my kanreki and my father's beiju. Left to right: Geoffrey (son-in-law), Shari (daughter), Yoshi (husband), me, Minoru (father), and Rose (mother).*

felt thanks to you, the reader, for your continued support. Please join me in carrying on the art of Japanese cuisine in our islands.

**Muriel Miura, CFCS**

# Introduction
## THE EVOLUTION
## OF JAPANESE FOOD, HAWAI'I-STYLE

By Arnold Hiura, *Food Historian*

*"Japanese Food, Hawai'i-Style is a genre of food that is unique unto itself. It has evolved and endured in people's kitchens for generations, largely unaffected by food trends from Japan, Hawai'i, or elsewhere around the globe."*

—Muriel Miura

Muriel Miura is the queen of local Japanese food, or, as she calls it, "Japanese food, Hawai'i-style." For more than five decades, Muriel has shared her knowledge of food via classes, television shows, and books. Throughout her journey, she has remained steadfast in her beliefs and principles as they relate to both cooking and life in general.

Hawai'i is a much different place now than it was in 1974 when Muriel first published her book, *Cook Japanese, Hawaiian Style*. Our culinary landscape, like everything else, is a constantly changing thing.

Look around. Today, Japanese food is fast gaining favor all around the world, and Hawai'i is no exception. And why should it be? Immigrants from Japan first settled in these islands some 150 years ago, and Hawai'i remains an immensely popular destination for millions of Japanese travelers each year. Sushi bars, izakaya (pubs), and noodle houses of many persuasions keep popping up at an amazing rate, along with elegant, high-end eateries bearing the names of some of Japan's most celebrated chefs.

In addition to the growing popularity of Japanese food, Hawai'i's local food scene in general is also riding its own tsunami of popularity. Spurred by the Hawai'i Regional Cuisine (HRC) revolution of the 1990s, a new generation of young, homegrown chefs is establishing its place alongside the HRC pioneers who inspired them.

None of this affects Muriel, who has seen her share of food fads come and go. "There are many examples of dishes and trends that were popular for a time, but nobody really talks about them anymore," she observes.

While she respects different styles of cooking, Muriel is simply being honest when she admits that she is not a huge fan of what has been termed "fusion" cuisine. "I prefer keeping things simple," she says. "I'm influenced by my father, I guess. He firmly believed that the true flavor of the ingredients should shine through."

The recipes that Muriel has chosen for this book emphasize economy and efficiency—two key components of local-style Japanese food. "Somehow, busy parents managed to feed large families that often numbered seven, eight, or nine children," she notes.

"This book is our effort to put in print the dishes we enjoyed as a family. I've tried to stick with the old recipes—the classics, as it were. These are the ones I believe are important to preserve—dishes that will stay with people."

## Immigration and Adaptation are Nearly Synonymous

*"The evolution began almost immediately ... the Japanese added their contributions to the local culture and were influenced by other ethnic groups in return."*
—Muriel Miura

How did Japanese food evolve to become part of the broader community? Muriel traces the roots of Hawai'i-style Japanese cuisine to the arrival of Japanese immigrants some 150 years ago. The first shipload of immigrants that landed in 1868 was followed by mass immigration from Japan beginning in 1885. Within a few years, Japanese comprised over 40 percent of the plantation workforce. Over the next decade, more than 20,000 Japanese had journeyed across the Pacific to work on Hawai'i's sugarcane plantations. By the time immigration from Japan was officially curtailed in 1924, more than 180,000 men, women, and children had emigrated from Japan to Hawai'i.

Most of them arrived with all of their worldly belongings in a single woven basket. Having signed three-year labor contracts, many planned to earn money to help their impoverished families in Japan and then return home. Due to various circumstances, however, most stayed.

With no money and no means of modern communication, these Issei (first-generation immigrants) had no choice but to quickly adapt to their new island home in the middle of the Pacific in order to survive. All immigrants—regardless of their place of origin—looked to the new land for opportunities. They also carried memories of their homelands in their hearts.

The fact that the Japanese arrived in such great numbers improved their odds of preserving and perpetuating cultural practices dear to them. Near the top of that list, of course, was food. Food was a daily challenge, as everyone had to eat in order to carry out their extremely strenuous work as field laborers, working from sunup to sundown, six days a week.

What they longed to eat was Japanese food—a diet based on rice accompanied by a variety of appropriately seasoned side dishes. Much of what they desired was not immediately available, of course, so everyone had to do the best they could with what was at hand.

Bacalhau, for example, the Portuguese word for salted cod, was one such plantation staple that people of all nationalities learned to incorporate into their diets. Other foods available to plantation workers at the time included such durable items as smoked meat, dried fish and shrimp, hard chorizo sausages, and pickled vegetables.

Salted, well-seasoned foods were popular because they did not spoil easily in Hawai'i's warm climate and, when prepared with vegetables, the flavors allowed a little okazu (entrée or side dish) to go a long way toward making a meal of rice more palatable.

Often, water was added to create soups and stews to stretch a family's food budget even further. Families tended vegetable gardens and foraged the upland forests for fern shoots and wild greens. Shoyu (soy sauce), miso, sugar, and vinegar were their preferred seasonings.

Coming from an island nation surrounded by the sea, the Japanese found their foodways had much in common with those of indigenous Hawaiians. Not only were they skilled fishermen, but they also viewed many varieties of seaweed, limpets, mollusks, and other sea creatures as delicacies.

Like the Hawaiians, the Japanese consumed fish—any fish—thoroughly from head to tail. Fresh fish was eaten raw, while others were salted and dried for consumption later. The only difference, it seemed, was that Hawaiians ate theirs with poi, while Japanese meals relied on rice.

## Plantation Life Mixes Things Up

*"For me, it all goes back to the plantation. The food starts to change in Hawai'i compared to Japan. The Issei came over with their own food culture and had to adapt to their new environment."*
—Muriel Miura

On Hawai'i's plantations, immigrants from China, Korea, the Philippines, Portugal, Puerto Rico, and other countries of origin lived and interacted. Many plantations were composed of separate ethnic camps. Some believe that being clustered in proximity to others who came from the same country allowed residents to better maintain their core cultural practices, such as language, festivals, religious practices, and, of course, food.

The Japanese, for example, observed traditional celebrations and festivals such as Oshogatsu (New Year's), Girl's Day, Boy's Day, and Obon (festival of the dead). Each event had its own special foods traditions.

Camps may have been segregated by ethnicity, but interaction between ethnic groups still occurred on a daily basis at work, at school, and on the playing fields. Again, food played an important role in fostering these relationships. One of the common practices on the plantation was for workers to share their food at lunchtime. Sharing lunches also took place among schoolchildren, although not to the same degree as was practiced by their parents at work.

*Japanese farmer in Hawai'i.* (Hawa'i State Archives)

"The Japanese brought bento box lunches with them from Japan. On the plantation, workers of different ethnic backgrounds would share their food with others. Many people consider the bento the forerunner to the local-style plate lunch," Muriel explains.

As it would be rude to refuse to eat someone else's food, over time this practice of sharing led people to expand their own culinary horizons and in some cases to adjust the balance of flavors in their cooking to better suit the tastes of their co-workers as well as the broader multi-ethnic population around them.

Although the food around it evolved, rice remained a constant. The Chinese preceded the Japanese to Hawai'i and had firmly established their preference for rice over other starchy staples such as taro, bread, sweet potatoes, or breadfruit. The indigenous Hawaiian population itself had been severely decimated by diseases, further contributing to the declining demand for poi. In the 1850s and '60s, taro patches were converted to rice cultivation. During this period, Hawai'i even exported some of its rice to California.

Ironically, the influx of Japanese immigrants eventually contributed to the demise of rice production in Hawai'i. Japanese preferred the short-grain rice that was grown in California over the long-grain varieties in Hawai'i. In addition, local farmers could not compete with the massive scale and mechanized production methods established by California growers.

Other than rice, workers of all ethnic backgrounds shared much in common when it came to food. They all made purchases at the general store. Workers kept vegetable gardens. A few raised chickens for eggs, while still others fished and hunted to augment their families' diets.

From time to time, someone raising chickens for eggs would thin their flock of less-productive birds. Or others ambitious enough to raise pigs or cows might slaughter an animal and sell or barter parts of it with others eager for fresh food.

Isolated towns or camps would be regularly serviced by traveling peddlers who would pack their specially equipped vehicles with fish, meat, vegetables, and tofu on ice and drive from place to place. Their visits were eagerly anticipated by loyal customers who had no means of transportation.

No matter how difficult life could get, an overriding sense of community came to characterize plantation life, and food was the glue that bound people together through hard times and helped to bridge the differences between various ethnic groups to create Hawai'i's multiethnic local culture.

## Urbanization and Diversification

*"Japanese moving off of the plantations
became an integral part of the society at large
... and so did their food."*
— Muriel Miura

After fulfilling their contractual obligations on the plantations, many Japanese began migrating to towns in pursuit of other forms of employment. Japanese quickly took on prominent roles as carpenters, storekeepers, blacksmiths, mechanics, restaurateurs, farmers, fishermen, barbers and hairdressers, tailors and seamstresses, and much more. They often formed ethnic communities such as Mō'ili'ili, Liliha, Kaimukī, Kalihi, Kaka'ako, and the 'A'ala district in downtown Honolulu, to name a few predominantly Japanese neighborhoods.

Local farmers grew what they could by way of fruits and vegetables, while others raised beef, pork, poultry, and eggs. The more entrepreneurial types opened stores or began manufacturing foodstuffs such as shoyu, sake, and tofu locally, while still others established trade companies to import desired items from Japan.

Japanese played an especially significant role in establishing, developing, and operating Hawai'i's commercial fishing industry, based on their knowledge and experiences in the seas around Japan. Besides the actual fishing, Japanese were deeply involved in the boat building, wholesale, and retail aspects of the industry.

As life for Hawai'i's Issei and Nisei (second generation) Japanese Americans grew more and more diverse, so did their food experiences. No longer restricted to rural plantation camps, they flourished in towns filled with stores, restaurants, and plate lunch wagons.

One of the prominent food establishments that characterized this era was the Japanese teahouse. Teahouses did not function quite like regular walk-in restaurants, but were popular sites to host special celebrations such as birthdays, anniversaries, and weddings. A typical, multi-course teahouse menu might include sashimi, miso soup, sushi, tempura, namasu, sukiyaki, crab, and teriyaki beef or chicken.

It is of particular note that Muriel's father, Minoru Kamada, acquired a teahouse in Pālama in 1945. The facility was being used as a rooming house at the time, but he converted it back to a teahouse known as Hananoya, or Paradise Garden. Muriel's father

*Mochizuki Tea House in Liliha.* (Honolulu Star-Advertiser)

was not a cook, but proved to be a fast learner. The teahouse also served as Muriel's introduction to cooking. "It was a place where people came to celebrate an occasion—weddings, mainly," she recalls. "Some business people would come. The waitresses wore kimonos and were called 'geishas.'"

More informal than teahouses were saimin stands that actually began on plantations and then fanned out to more urban settings. "Saimin" is actually a Chinese word and is likely Chinese in origin, or at least in inspiration. However, this simple noodle soup—distinguished by its chewy curly noodles and dashi (broth)—is more closely tied to Japanese-run establishments on the plantations. Selling saimin at 10 cents a bowl, neighborhood stands began opening throughout the Islands in the 1930s. Regardless of its exact ethnic origin or location, saimin is easily one of Hawai'i's all time favorite comfort foods.

Another type of food establishment that carried over from plantations to towns is the okazuya, or what some describe as a "Japanese delicatessen." According to *The Okazu Guide*, its origins date back to early Japanese workers. By 1900, the *Guide* claims more than a hundred Japanese okazuya were spread throughout the islands.

The proliferation of okazuya bears testament to the popularity of these places among all ethnic groups. Common okazuya food choices reflect a wide range of ethnic dishes and unique local favorites: inarizushi (cone sushi), fried chicken, shoyu hot dogs, mac salad, namasu, sweet potato tempura, and chow fun were some standard okazuya dishes.

"There is no doubt that okazuya are unique to Hawai'i," the *Guide* states. Compared to Japanese food in Japan, the Hawai'i versions have their own unique flavor profiles, usually much sweeter. Special recipes have been developed by family-run okazuya and passed down from generation to generation.

## World War II: Learning to "Make Do"

*"Everything changed during the war; a lot of things were rationed. There was a scarcity of food, scarcity of certain ingredients. People had to improvise and innovate because they had nothing."*
— Muriel Miura

When World War II broke out, Hawai'i was designated a war zone and placed under military rule. Strictly enforced lackouts, curfews, rationing, and shortages of various goods were all part of life in Hawai'i during the war.

"You couldn't get many ingredients, like when my mother wanted to make makizushi (sushi rolls), we couldn't get nori," Muriel recalls. Japanese goods in general were cut off. "We were craving makizushi—any kind of makizushi—so much that we used won bok

(Chinese cabbage) instead of nori. We blanched the cabbage leaves and rolled the sushi rice and fillings inside."

During the war, foods such as poi, beans, Vienna sausage, and Spam® became commonplace, Muriel states. "We were very fortunate, though, because my family did not go hungry like some other families. My mother's brothers were farmers. One uncle raised chickens another raised pigs. During the war, everything was rationed—even meat. It was hard to get meat. Every so often my uncles would slaughter a pig and bring it to my grandma's house. The carcass would be laid out on the dining room table and my uncles would cut it all up. Everybody had a little bit of pork."

In addition, Muriel's grandfather was a fisherman who would catch ahi and bring home fish. "He would sell the good parts, of course, so we would eat all the scrap pieces: the head, the belly... We would chop up the head of the fish and cook it up with ginger and shoyu." The head of the fish is very meaty, and fish eaters love it, Muriel adds. "We called it 'ara,' referring to the fish head, bones, fins. We would either cook it with shoyu, sugar and ginger, or use it to make soup."

As a child, Muriel also remembers buying snacks from the "anpan man," who sold pastries and baked goods from his car. "We had no chocolates, so we used to climb the tamarind tree and pick the fruit. We'd suck on the tamarinds and pretend that they were crack seed."

Ice cakes were an economical snack. Muriel's mother would freeze milk, sugar, and vanilla in an ice cube tray. Sometimes, left-over coffee was also made into ice cakes, she recalls.

Under a shroud of suspicion following the bombing of Pearl Harbor, Japanese-Americans worked with heightened vigilance to demonstrate their unswerving loyalty to America. Thousands of island G.I.s—many of them Nisei—volunteered for military service and left the familiar surroundings of their island homes for the first time. They traveled across the U.S. mainland and Europe; others served in Asia and elsewhere in the Pacfic. Meanwhile, nearly one million U.S. soldiers and civilian personnel passed through the islands as part of the war effort.

Such momentous events could not help but make a significant impact on society. The full effect of these activities would become more apparent after war's end, including the influences on local food. Being "American," after all, meant sharing in the American Dream, replete with hamburgers, hot dogs, sodas, milk shakes, and whatever those new-fangled television sets portrayed America to be.

## Postwar: Plate Lunch Paradise

Nothing could be more American than the iconic drive-in restaurant, and Hawai'i had its share of these. Some even had car hops doling out milk shakes, hamburgers, hot dogs, and sodas. Drive-ins rose to popularity in the 1950s, largely on the popularity of their local-style plate lunches and saimin in addition to burgers and fries.

The success of the plate lunch was its ability to pair foods that people liked with rice and macaroni salad. Food could not be too exotic, like natto (fermented soybeans). What evolved into plate lunch classics were foods that appealed to the broadest cross-section of Hawai'i's people. One magazine polled its readers to see what the top plate lunch dishes were. Making the list were: laulau, chicken katsu, poke, loco moco, kālua pig, teriyaki beef (or chicken), beef stew, hamburger steak, and chicken hekka.

Other all-time local favorites with ties to Japanese culture are shave ice and Spam® musubi. The American-style snow cone is really crushed ice. It's not finely shaved as it's made here. "We used to have maybe three or four flavors," Muriel reflects. "Now they have a myriad of flavors."

Spam® musubi can be found nearly everywhere—even convenience stores and gas stations. "It's become the go-to snack," Muriel notes. "It's even a big deal on the mainland." While people in Hawai'i firmly claim Spam® musubi as their own, there are those who will argue that its origins can be traced to World War II internment camps on the mainland.

## The Spirit of 'Ohana

*"One thing that all ethnic groups shared in common was a strong sense of family bonds."*

— Muriel Miura

This book is filled with Muriel's family's tried-and-true recipes. She learned most of them from her father. These recipes are very simple—the type of dishes that people made everyday to feed their families. People in Hawai'i always prefer informal over formal lifestyles, like comfortable clothing and simple food.

"Ever since I was a young girl, our family would gather every Sunday for potluck dinner," Muriel says. "We cooked and got together. Everyone sat around and talked story. It was not how fancy the food was, but that it was done well.

Mom would prepare chicken hekka on Sundays. I started cooking with my dad when I was still a kid at the teahouse. Although that lasted for about a year, it piqued my father's interest in Japanese food and continued over into the years cooking for our family's Sunday dinners. We cooked together on Sundays. He would tell me stories—tidbits about what they ate when they were kids. He was so poor, living with his mother in Yamaguchi, Japan. They fashioned most of their of their meals from kuzu (rubbish parts). They could not afford white rice."

Family gathered every Sunday to share a potluck meal and spend some time together, but it was more for the relationships than it was the food.

## Preserving the Legacy

*"This book is for the young generation. The stories of their forbears are told in these dishes. Perhaps the flavors will open up their connection to their past."*
— Muriel Miura

In Japan, the term washoku refers to traditional Japanese food— simple, home-cooked fare. It does not include the type of food served in fancy restaurants. In 2013, washoku was granted official UNESCO (United Nations Educational, Scientific, and Cultural Organization) Intangible Cultural Heritage of Humanity status. One of the reasons for this action is the concern that modern Japan is losing its traditional Japanese cuisine.

Like Muriel advocating local-style cooking at home, those who champion the cause of washoku see the connection between food and culture. Does its decline, they wonder, reflect the changing values of Japanese families?

Like Japanese food Hawai'i-style, washoku is rather difficult to define. At its most basic, it is described as a meal based on rice, served along with soups, side dishes, and tsukemono (pickles). Sound familiar? Other definitions of washoku describe its emphasis on the natural flavors of food. The goal, it says, is to enhance, not mask, each ingredient. Food should be both healthy and delicious, simple and sophisticated, all at the same time.

The Japanese term umami (loosely defined as "savory") has gained great traction in recent years. It is one of the core principles of traditional washoku cooking, which aims to subtly and skillfully combine sweet, sour, salty, and bitter simply and economically.

The fundamentals of washoku, one might argue, were transplanted to Hawai'i by immigrants over a century ago. Family cooks were key in perpetuating it and reinterpreting it to fit the local lifestyle. Like washoku, local-style Japanese food represents our ties with the past and to the memory of those pioneers who sacrificed their own lives to make ours better.

Life has changed since those early days. The ease of travel, population growth, intermarriage, and global communications all underscore Hawai'i's ever-expanding, multi-ethnic banquet table.

"Our children and their children move away; their worlds are different," Muriel says. "We hope they will work hard, find success, find happiness … but will they ever know the lifestyle we did? Will they ever know how it is to live in a place where people trusted each other and relied on each other? Maybe not. If not, then maybe these flavors will help to open up their connection to their past. Maybe we will preserve some of the Japanese culture in our own little way."

In this book, Muriel has chosen her most prized family recipes. "It's important to preserve these memories—the experiences that are told in these dishes," she says. "I would like my daughter, her son and daughter—all three of them—to go to the kitchen and make something together. And I hope that, someday, my grandkids will teach someone else something—one dish, one thing …"

Muriel often alludes to a familiar Japanese saying: Kodomo no tame ni (for the sake of the children). "I see this as a legacy piece dedicated to my daughter and my grandchildren," she concludes. "Hopefully, others will view it in a similar vein."

# Bento & Zensai
# Box Lunches & Appetizers

In the early 1900s the word "zensai" was coined by Kitaoji Rosanjin, a famous potter, to mean "appetizer." Elegant zensai are served in tiny portions to whet the appetite. Because of their versatility, many dishes in this section can also be served as side dishes or other courses for a Japanese-style meal.

Numerous dishes featured throughout this book may also be packed in attractive compartmentalized "bento boxes" featuring a generous portion of cooked rice with a variety of side dishes such as meat, seafood, braised vegetables, sweet omelet, and pickles. The "obento" is the Japanese version of Hawai'i's fast food/plate lunch with an entirely new meaning.

# Gyuniku No Teriyaki Dango
## Teriyaki Meatballs

*Yield: About 30 cocktail meatballs*

**G**round chicken may be substituted for beef to form the meatballs. Seasoned with a delectable sauce, this dish is an excellent appetizer as well as an excellent entrée.

½ **pound lean ground beef**
1 **egg**
1 **tablespoon bread crumbs**
2 **tablespoons chopped onion**
⅛ **teaspoon pepper**

*Sauce:*
½ **cup shoyu**
¼ **cup sugar**
2 **tablespoons sake (rice wine)**
1 **teaspoon fresh grated ginger**
1 **clove garlic, crushed**

**Minced green onion, optional**

Combine first 5 ingredients, mix well and shape into ¾-inch meatballs. Place in skillet or chafing dish. Mix together ingredients for Sauce and pour over meatballs. Simmer over medium-low heat for 20 minutes. Garnish with minced green onion, if desired. Serve hot.

# Teriyaki Gyuniku No Kushi Sashi
## Shari's Teri Beef on a Stick

*Yield: 4 to 6 servings*

As youngsters, we always ordered tasty sticks of "barbecue meat" to accompany our bowls of saimin whenever we had lunch at the saimin stand in Kaka'ako.

**1 pound top round or sirloin, cut into 1 × 5-inch strips**
**Bamboo skewers, soaked in water for 30 minutes**

### *Teriyaki Sauce:*
**½ cup water**
**½ cup shoyu**
**¼ cup brown sugar, packed**
**1 tablespoon grated fresh ginger**
**1 clove garlic, crushed**
**¼ cup mirin (sweet rice wine) or sake (rice wine)**

Thread beef on skewers. Combine Teriyaki Sauce ingredients and mix well; marinate beef 15 to 30 minutes. Broil in preheated broiler compartment or cook on hibachi or outdoor grill for 3 to 4 minutes or until of desired doneness. Baste frequently.

# Kani Tamago Maki
## Crab Egg Roll

*Yield: About 8 to 12 pieces*

*T*amago maki is a popular appetizer, as well a favorite side dish. It also serves as a lovely garnish in bento boxes.

  **2 eggs**
  **½ teaspoon salt**
  **¼ cup minced green onion**
  **¼ cup crab★, minced**
  **2 tablespoons oil**

Combine first 4 ingredients; mix well. Cook one-half of egg mixture in 1 tablespoon of hot oil. Roll egg, like you would jelly roll. Prepare another roll, using remaining ingredients. Cool and slice into 1½-inch pieces. Serve with mayonnaise or shoyu, if desired.

★Cold cuts may be substituted for crab.

## Rumaki

*Yield: About 32 pieces*

*T*here was a time when this appetizer was always on the pūpū menu at local gatherings.

  **1 (10-ounce) package frozen chicken livers**
  **¼ cup butter or margarine**
  **16 slices bacon**
  **32 water chestnuts**

Defrost chicken livers and cut each section into 4 pieces. Sauté in butter or margarine for 1 to 2 minutes, or until golden brown on the outside, but not cooked through. Cut bacon slices in half. Wrap liver section and 1 water chestnut in ½ bacon slice and secure with cocktail pick. Broil 3 to 5 minutes on each side, or until brown. Serve hot.

# Butaniku Konbu Maki
## Pork Seaweed Roll

*Yield: About 30 cocktail pieces*

**K**onbu maki is one of the traditional items you will find in a lacquered Jubako during New Year celebrations.

**8 ounces nishime konbu**
**1 pound pork, cut into**
  **½ × ½ × 2½-inch strips**
**Kampyo (dried gourd)**
  **or string to tie**
**2½ cups water**
**⅓ cup shoyu**
**½ teaspoon salt**
**¼ cup sugar**
**1 tablespoon sake**
  **(rice wine)**

Soak konbu in warm water to cover; wash sand off and cut into 5- or 6-inch lengths. Place a piece of pork on one end of the konbu strip, roll as you would jelly roll and tie with kampyo or string.

### Bento

Bento is a single portion take-out or home-packed meal common in Japanese cuisine. The bento box generally holds rice, fish or meat, pickles or cooked vegetables usually arranged in some kind of box. Similar forms of boxed lunches are found in other Asian countries and Hawai'i has adopted a localized version of bento featuring local tastes after more than a century of Japanese influence in the islands. It is the predecessor of Hawai'i's plate lunches, says a food historian.

Place the konbu maki in a saucepan, add water and cook until tender, about 1½ to 2 hours, over low heat.

Add shoyu, salt, sugar, and sake; cook for additional 30 minutes.

# Katsuo/Maguro Butsu
## Aku/'Ahi (Tuna) Poke
*Yield: 6 to 8 servings*

When preparing big fish like tuna for sashimi, the Japanese fishmongers cut the flesh lengthwise into long rectangular shapes. After the prime parts are cut out, the remaining trimmings are sold for less. These cube-chopped trimmings are referred to as "butsu," which has all the qualities of the best tuna sashimi. To those of us in Hawai'i, it is simply "poke."

**2 pounds aku or 'ahi fillet, cubed**
**1 cup chopped ogo (seaweed)**
**Hawaiian rock salt, to taste**
**½ teaspoon dried chili peppers, coarsely chopped**
**1 teaspoon sesame oil**
**'Inamona (roasted kukui nut, pounded and salted),**
   **to taste, optional**

Combine fish with ogo, tossing gently to combine. Add remaining ingredients.

## Variations:
- Season with soy sauce, minced ginger, minced green onion, red peppers, and/or thin slices of sweet onion instead of Hawaiian salt, sesame oil, and 'inamona.
- Poke can be made with imitation crab, limu, aburage (fried bean curd), king clam, or octopus instead of raw fish.
- ***Spicy Maguro Butsu:***
      1 pound 'ahi fillet, cubed
      1 tablespoon shoyu or to taste
      ½ tablespoon sesame oil
      2 tablespoons mayonnaise
      1 tablespoon sriracha or to taste
      1 tablespoon minced green onion, optional
      2 to 3 thin slices sweet onion, optional
      2 teaspoons tobiko (fish roe), optional

# Ebi No Nitsuke
## Teriyaki Shrimp

*Yield: 4 to 6 servings*

**S**imply seasoned with teriyaki sauce, this shrimp dish is easily prepared and is especially popular with young adults.

**1 pound fresh frozen shrimps in shell**

**Sauce:**
   **¼ cup sake (rice wine)**
   **¼ cup shoyu**
   **3 tablespoons sugar**
   **2 tablespoons water**

Rinse shrimps, combine sauce ingredients and cook shrimps over medium heat 3 to 5 minutes or until done. Serve hot or cold.

# Tamago Maki
## Egg Roll

*Yield: 12 one-inch egg rolls*

*E*veryone loves an omelet, especially if it is beautifully rolled, sliced, and arranged artistically on a lovely platter.

### Egg Sheets:
  2 eggs
  ½ teaspoon salt
  1 tablespoon cornstarch

### Pork Hash Filling:
  ½ pound ground pork
  1 tablespoon minced green onion
  ½ teaspoon sugar
  ½ teaspoon salt
  1 teaspoon shoyu
  ½ teaspoon sake (rice wine)
  1 slice ginger, crushed

Combine ingredients for egg sheets and fry tissue paper thin in square skillet, or if a round skillet is used, cut off rounded edges to make squares. Makes 2 sheets.

Combine ingredients for Pork Hash Filling and mix well. Place on egg sheets and spread evenly, leaving 1 inch from the far edge clear. Roll from the end closest to you and fasten ends with cornstarch paste. Cut each roll into 6 pieces. Wrap in double thickness of cheesecloth. Steam 15 to 20 minutes.

# Horenso No Tamago Maki
## Spinach-Egg Roll
*Yield: 8 to 12 pieces*

*U*sing one's imagination, an endless variety of omelets can be created and served to guests as appetizers or side dishes.

### Shoyu Sauce:
**3 tablespoons shoyu**
**2 tablespoons sugar**
**1 teaspoon sake (rice wine)**

**1 box frozen spinach**
**4 eggs**

**Oil for frying**

Combine Shoyu Sauce ingredients and stir until sugar dissolves. Partially thaw spinach. Cook in ½ cup of boiling water for 10 minutes. Gently squeeze out excess water then marinate in sauce for 1 hour; set aside.

Combine eggs; beat well. Fry half of beaten eggs in 1 tablespoon hot oil to form a thin sheet. When eggs are almost done, place half of marinated spinach along one side of egg sheet. Roll as in jelly roll. Let Spinach-Egg Roll cook for a short while after rolling. Remove from pan and cut into 1½-inch slices. Cook remaining portion in the same manner.

# Ika No Su-Miso
## Squid with Miso Dip

*Yield: About 12 servings*

The unique flavor of squid is delicately enhanced by the Miso Sauce. As an exotic item, it may even turn out to be the talk of the evening!

**2 pounds squid, cleaned**
**1 pound green onion, blanched**

*Miso Sauce:*
  **½ cup miso**
  **¼ cup sugar**
  **2 tablespoons rice vinegar**
  **1 teaspoon mirin (sweet rice wine)**
  **½ teaspoon grated fresh ginger**

Wash and drain squid. Slice into ½-inch crosswise pieces. Cook in water to cover for 5 minutes, or until done. Drain and chill thoroughly.

Cut green onion into 1-inch pieces. Combine Miso Sauce ingredients and mix well. Add squid and onion to Miso Sauce; mix well.

# Gyoza
## Pork Pot Stickers

*Yield: Approximately 3 dozen*

The pork filling for this popular dumpling may be substituted with ground chicken. This dish is often served as a side with ramen or other noodle dishes.

**Filling:**
   ¼ **pound ground pork**
   ½ **pound ground beef**
   **1 egg, beaten**
   **2 dried shiitake (mushrooms),**
      **softened in water and minced**
   ¼ **teaspoon salt**
   **1 tablespoon shoyu**
   **1 tablespoon mirin (sweet rice wine)**
   ¼ **teaspoon sesame seed oil**
   **2 tablespoons minced green onion or chives**
   **1 cup finely minced cabbage, optional**

   **3 dozen gyoza no kawa (won ton pi or gyoza wrappers)**
   **1 quart canola oil for frying**

Combine filling ingredients and mix thoroughly.

To make a pot sticker: Fill each gyoza wrapper with 1 tablespoon filling mixture. Moisten edges of wrapper. Fold in half and flute edges to seal.

Fry in oil heated to 365°F for 1 to 2 minutes or until golden brown. Gyoza may also be steam-fried for 20 to 30 minutes instead. Drain on absorbent paper and serve with purchased ponzu or shoyu, if desired make Ponzu Sauce (see page 72).

# Dashi & Owanrui
## Soup Stocks & Soups

Dashi, soup stock, is the basis for delicate Japanese soups, simmered dishes, and sauces. The most common dashi is made from dashi konbu and katsuobushi (tuna flakes). Dashi can be refrigerated or frozen. Frozen dashi cubes come in handy when you need small amounts for cooking.

Two kinds of soups are served by the Japanese:
- **Clear Soup**: made from konbu, dried fish, slightly seasoned fish, shrimp, or chicken and some seasonal vegetables.
- **Thick Soup**: made from soup stock and seasoned with miso (soybean paste). Vegetables, chicken, pork, fish, and shellfish are sometimes added.

### *Ichiban Dashi*
# Basic Soup Stock
*Yield: About 2½ to 3 quarts*

*T*he simplest dashi is made with only konbu (kelp), but katsuobushi (dried bonito flakes) or dried sardines are usually added to enhance its flavor. Dried shiitake mushrooms also make excellent stock suitable for vegetarians. Dashi-no-moto (instant dashi powder) may be substituted.

>    **3 quarts water**
>    **1 (4-inch) square dashi konbu**
>    **1 cup katsuobushi (dried fish flakes)**

Bring water to a boil. Add konbu, let water come to a boil again; remove konbu and set aside. Add katsuobushi; turn heat off and let stand 5 minutes. Strain, using double thickness of cheesecloth. Use stock for soup base or in the preparation of numerous Japanese dishes.

**Tip:** Do not boil the dashi after adding the kelp or bonito as the delicate flavor of the stock will be altered and become too strong.

## *Niban Dashi*
# Basic Stock for Vegetables
### *Yield: About 5 cups*

**S**econd-quality stocks like Niban Dashi and stronger stocks can be used for noodle broths, dipping sauces, stews or simmering vegetables. Dashi can be refrigerated or frozen into cubes for later use.

> 5½ cups water
> 1 (4-inch) square dashi konbu
> 1 cup cooked katsuobushi (from Ichiban Dashi; see previous page)
> ½ cup katsuobushi (dried fish flakes)

Add konbu and katsuobushi to water; bring to a boil over high heat. Reduce heat and simmer, uncovered, for 5 minutes. Strain, using double thickness of cheesecloth. Discard konbu and katsuobushi. Use stock for vegetable and other main dishes—i.e., shabu shabu, nishime, umani, etc.

## *Dashi-no-Moto*
# Instant Soup Stock

**T**he development of dashi-no-moto (instant soup powder) has greatly simplified Japanese cooking and is an acceptable substitute for dashi. I've seen cooks sprinkle some of the powder directly into stir-fry dishes as a seasoning.

| # cups dashi = | # cups water + | # teaspoons dashi-no-moto |
|---|---|---|
| 4 cups | 4 cups | 2½ teaspoons (1 pkg.) |
| 3 cups | 3 cups | 1¾ teaspoons |
| 2 cups | 2 cups | 1¼ teaspoons |
| 1½ cups | 1½ cups | ¾ teaspoon |
| 1 cup | 1 cup | ½ teaspoon |

Use the table above to obtain your desired amount of dashi by combining the indicated amounts of water and dashi-no-moto.

# *Osumashi*
# Clear Soup

*Yield: 6 to 8 servings*

Peering into a bowl of Osumashi is like viewing nature's artistry in miniature so the flavor should be delicate and refined. The preparation of soup in Japan can be an art in itself and often the measure of a good cook.

> **6 cups water**
> **½ cup dried shrimps**
> **1 (2 × 6-inch) piece dashi konbu, optional**
> **1 teaspoon salt**
> **1 teaspoon shoyu**

> *Garnishes:*
> **Minced green onion**
> **Tofu cubes**
> **Peas**
> **Snow peas, slivered**

Combine first three ingredients. Bring water to a boil, remove konbu. Simmer 15 to 20 minutes. Add remaining ingredients. Turn heat off; strain before serving. Garnish with green onion, tofu cubes, peas, or slivers of snow peas.

## Variation:

**Kakitama Jitue (Scrambled Egg Soup):** Add beaten egg slowly, stirring constantly, into boiling soup. Garnish with minced green onion, if desired.

## Miso Shiru
# Soybean Paste Soup

*Yield: 6 to 8 servings*

**M**iso Shiru, with an egg cooked in it, is one of the true flavors of Japan to me. It is a favorite breakfast dish for many—served with rice, perhaps a piece of grilled fish and pickles.

> **6 cups Dashi (see options on pages 14-15)**
> **6 to 8 tablespoons miso**
> **"Tane" of choice (main ingredients, see below)**
> **¼ cup minced green onion**

> ### Recommended "tane" combinations:
> **Tofu cubes and wakame (seaweed)**
> **Sliced bamboo shoots, wakame, and snow peas**
> **Aburage (fried bean curd) and satoimo (dasheen)**
> **Tofu cubes and horenso (spinach) leaves**

Bring dashi to a boil; add miso and simmer 10 to 15 minutes. Add "tane" of choice; cook additional minute or until heated through. Serve hot, garnished with green onion.

# Sakana No Suimono
## Fish Cake Soup

*Yield: 4 to 6 servings*

*J*apanese meals almost always include a comforting soup and what can be easier to make than this one!

**½ pound prepared raw fish cake paste**
**6 cups boiling water**
**1 teaspoon lemon juice**
**¼ teaspoon julienned lemon rind**
**1 teaspoon shoyu**
**¼ teaspoon salt (or as desired)**

### *Garnishes:*
**2 tablespoons minced green onion**
**Lemon zest**

Drop fish cake into boiling water by spoonfuls; simmer until fish cake rises to surface. Add remaining ingredients. Top with green onion and lemon zest.

## *Chiri*
# Fish and Tofu Soup
*Yield: 6 to 8 servings*

This delicate soup, called *Chiri*, is almost as popular as *Miso Soup*. The soup base is made of fish and konbu with cubes of tofu added. Serve in covered lacquer soup bowls and the soup will be kept hot by a vacuum created when the lid is put on the bowl. To remove the lid, squeeze the bowl lightly to release.

> **1 pound fish fillet or fish bone**
> **3-inch piece dashi konbu, optional**
> **6 cups boiling water**
> **1 tablespoon lemon juice**
> **1 teaspoon salt**
> **1 tablespoon shoyu**
> **½ block tofu, cut into cubes**
>
> **<u>Garnishes:</u>**
> **½ cup minced green onion**
> **1 tablespoon lemon rind, slivered**

Cut fish into strips. Add fish or fish bones and konbu to boiling water; simmer 10 to 15 minutes. Remove konbu; add lemon juice, salt, shoyu, and tofu. Cook additional minute or until tofu is heated through. Garnish with green onion and lemon rind.

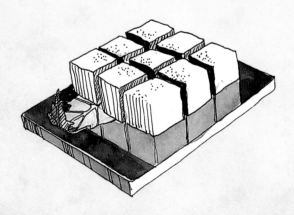

## *Ozoni*
# New Year's Soup
### *Yield: 6 servings*

**O**zoni is traditionally served on New Year's Day. Each district of Japan, and family, has its own variant of this dish, the only constant being that this soup always includes a piece of mochi.

> 1 pound boneless chicken, cut into bite-size pieces
> 6 cups boiling water
> 1 teaspoon salt
> 1 teaspoon shoyu
> 1 dried shiitake (mushroom), softened in water and slivered
> 6 pieces mochi (glutinous rice cake)
> 12 thin slices kamaboko (steamed fish cake)
> ½ bunch mizuna (Japanese cabbage), blanched and cut into 1½-inch pieces

Simmer chicken in water for 20 to 30 minutes; add salt, soy sauce, and shiitake; simmer additional minute.

Broil mochi until puffed and soft. Arrange kamaboko, greens, and mochi in individual soup bowls and slowly pour hot soup over arrangement. Serve immediately.

# *Gohanmono*
# Rice Dishes

Rice is the essence of Japanese cooking. Almost every dish in Japanese cuisine is designed to accompany a bowl of carefully prepared rice. Rice was introduced to Japan either directly from China or via the Korean peninsula during the prehistoric era—as long ago as the thirteenth century, BC. By the sixth century, rice had become firmly established as a staple food of Japan and remains so to this day.

This chapter features some classics, as well as contemporary, nutritious rice dishes, which are meals in themselves.

Rice is economical, delicious, nutritious, and versatile. It is without any doubt your most useful food. More than 7,000 varieties of rice are produced throughout the world but we need only concern ourselves with the following:

- **Long-grain rice**: Its length is four to five times its width; the grains are clear and translucent and they remain distinct and separate after cooking.
- **Medium-grain rice**: Its length is three times its width. It is slightly less expensive than long-grain because it requires a shorter growing season and produces higher yields per acre.
- **Short-grain rice**: Its length is one and a half to two times as long as its width. This is the variety preferred by the Japanese.
- **Brown rice**: The whole, unpolished grain, with only the outer, inedible, fibrous hull removed. Requires more water and longer cooking than white rice and has a chewy texture and nutty flavor.

- **Regular milled white rice:** Hulls, germ, outer bran layers, and most of the inner bran are removed in the milling process. It is bland in flavor and fluffy when cooked. This type of rice is also reinforced with vitamins lost in the milling process.
- **Precooked rice (quick type)**: Completely cooked and needs only to stand in boiling water to prepare.
- **Parboiled rice**: Cooked before milling by steam pressure, which aids in the retention of much of the natural vitamins and minerals. It requires a longer cooking period than regular milled white rice. The grains are fluffy and plump when cooked.
- **Wild rice**: Not rice at all but the seed of a wild grass found around the Great Lakes region. It is much more expensive than the other types of rice.

TO TINT RICE: Add few drops of food coloring to liquid in which rice is to be cooked.

TO FREEZE RICE: Place cooked rice in freezer containers; seal and label. Store up to eight months at zero degrees or less. Thaw and reheat by cooking with a few tablespoons of water in covered saucepan or use for fried rice and casserole dishes. Rice reheats well in the microwave.

TO REFRIGERATE RICE: Place in airtight container; rice will keep for about one week. Resteam, reheat, or use for fried rice or casserole dishes.

COOKING YIELD OF RICE:
- 1 cup uncooked brown rice yields 3½ cups cooked
- 1 cup uncooked regular white milled rice yields 3 cups cooked
- 1 cup uncooked parboiled rice yields 3 cups cooked
- 1 cup uncooked precooked rice yields a little more than 2 cups cooked

## *Gohan*
# Steamed Rice

*Yield: 4 to 6 servings*

**T**he Japanese prefer Japonica medium- and short-grain rice to other varieties. As rice is served at each Japanese-style meal its proper preparation is extremely important. It is not unusual for a cook's talent be judged by the quality of the steamed rice served.

**2 cups rice**
**2¼ cups water**

Wash and drain rice. Add water; cover and let stand 1 hour. Bring water to a boil, reduce heat to simmer, and continue to simmer until water level equals rice level; about 5 minutes. Reduce heat to low and cook additional 15 to 20 minutes. Turn heat off. Leave cover on and let steam 10 minutes before serving.

## *Okayu*
# Rice Gruel

*Yield: 4 servings*

**G**randma and Mom's remedy for when we felt "delicate or sick" was always a bowl of this hot rice gruel with umeboshi (pickled plum). It was also served with crumbled, toasted nori (seaweed) or a sprinkled of bonito flakes.

**6 cups water**
**1 cup rice, washed and drained**

Soak rice in water 2 to 3 hours. Bring water to boil; simmer over low heat for 45 to 50 minutes or until rice is very soft and gruel is thick.

*Imo-Gai*

# Rice in Tea with Sweet Potato

*Yield: 4 to 6 servings*

*T*his was one of Dad's comfort foods that was frequently on the menu at our home ... I especially enjoyed the sweet potatoes in it. Mom used to substitute lima beans for sweet potatoes sometimes.

**1 tablespoon green tea leaves**
**9 cups water**
**1 medium sweet potato, peeled and cut into bite-size pieces, optional**
**¾ cup rice, washed and drained**

Place tea in bag or tea ball and immerse in water. Bring water to boil; add sweet potato and cook 5 minutes. Add rice; cook over high heat 12 to 15 minutes or until rice is cooked, but firm. DO NOT OVERCOOK. Remove tea bag and serve hot.

*Variation:*

**Cha-Gai (Rice in Tea):** Omit sweet potato

*Tori Gohan*

# Chicken Rice

*Yield: 4 to 6 servings*

A Japanese version of a meal in a pot is made when the rice is cooked with bits meat and some vegetables. Just add a side dish or two, pickled vegetables and a cup of hot green tea to complete the menu.

**1 large dried shiitake (mushroom)**
**½ cup hot water**
**2 cups rice, washed and drained**
**1½ cups water**
**¼ cup mirin (sweet rice wine)**
**1 cup boneless chicken, sliced**
**½ cup carrot, slivered**
**2 teaspoons shoyu**
**¼ teaspoon salt**

Soak dried mushroom in ½ cup hot water to soften. Slice mushroom.

Combine mushroom soaking liquid with remaining ingredients. Stir slightly to combine. Bring to a boil in covered pot; simmer 5 minutes. Cook over low heat additional 15 to 20 minutes or until rice is cooked. Turn heat off, leaving cover on. Let stand and steam 5 minutes. Garnish with blanched Chinese peas, if desired.

## Variation:
**Matsutake Gohan (Mushroom Rice):** Increase mushroom to 2 and delete chicken and carrot from recipe. Prepare as directed above.

Note: This recipe may be prepared in the rice cooker following the manufacturer's directions.

## *Maze Gohan*
# Mixed Rice

*Yield: 6 to 8 servings*

*V*egetables, julienned and usually combined with dried shrimp, are simmered and seasoned to perfection in a delicious broth, then tossed with freshly cooked hot rice. It is very similar to Bara (scattered) Sushi except the rice is not flavored with sushi vinegar.

**9 cups hot cooked rice**

### *Vegetables (Gu):*
**½ konnyaku (tuber root flour cake), minced**
**1 small carrot, slivered**
**3 dried shiitake (mushrooms), softened in water and slivered**
**½ cup gobo (burdock root), slivered**
**⅓ block kamaboko (steamed fish cake), slivered**
**1½ cups water**
**6 green beans (string), slivered**

### *Seasonings:*
**1 tablespoon dried shrimp**
**¼ cup sugar**
**1 teaspoon salt**
**¼ cup shoyu**

### *Garnishes (optional):*
**Fried egg strips**
**Nori strips**

Combine Vegetable (Gu) ingredients, except green beans, simmer 3 to 5 minutes, or until vegetables are tender. Add beans and Seasonings; cook additional 3 to 5 minutes. Drain and cool.

Mix into cooked rice. Garnish with fried egg and/or nori strips, if desired. Serve hot.

## Oyako Donburi
# Rice with Chicken and Egg Topping
### *Yield: 4 to 6 servings*

*O*onburi is a deep bowl with a lid used for "donburi-mono," which is hot cooked rice topped with meat, fish, egg or vegetables, drizzled with a sauce to flavor the rice. Mom frequently made this dish, as it is a typical Japanese "meal in one." Simply delicious!

**1 pound boneless chicken, cut into thin slivers**
**4½ cups chicken broth**
**6 small bamboo shoots, slivered**
**1 medium round onion, cut into thin slices**
**2 teaspoons salt**
**2 teaspoons sugar**
**2 tablespoons shoyu**
**¼ cup mirin (sweet rice wine)**
**½ cup minced green onion**
**6 eggs, beaten**

**9 cups hot cooked rice**

> ### Mirin
> This sweet cooking rice wine is an important ingredient in most Japanese recipes.

### Garnish:
**Toasted ajitsuke (flavored) nori**

Simmer chicken in broth for 5 minutes. Add next six ingredients; bring to a boil. Add green onion. Pour beaten egg over chicken mixture. Cover and cook over low heat for 30 seconds. Serve in individual bowls over hot rice. Garnish with crushed, toasted nori (seaweed), if desired.

### Variation:
**Itoko Donburi (Rice with Beef and Egg Topping):** Substitute ½ pound beef cut into thin strips for chicken.

*Tendon*

# Rice with Tempura Topping

*Yield: 4 to 6 servings*

A bowl of steaming, hot cooked rice topped with your favorite tempura and tempura sauce drizzled atop. Awesome!

**6 cups hot cooked rice**
**12 jumbo or 18 medium shrimp tempura (see page 119)**

*Tare (Sauce):*
**1 cup Dashi (see options on pages 14-15)**
**2 teaspoons shoyu**
**2 teaspoons sugar**
**½ teaspoon sake (rice wine)**

Place hot cooked rice in 4- to 6-inch donburi (Japanese bowl).

Place prepared shrimp tempura over hot rice. Combine Tare ingredients and pour ¼ cup over shrimps to serve. Serve hot.

*Variations:*
- **Katsu Don:** Place prepared Tonkatsu (see page 131) or Chicken Katsu (see page 133) on hot rice and serve with tonkatsu sauce drizzled over or on side.
- **Yakitori Don:** Place cooked Yakitori (see page 160) or Teriyaki Chicken (see page 154) on hot rice and serve with teriyaki sauce drizzled over.
- **Poke Don:** Place Poke of choice (see page 6) over Sushi Rice (see page 41) or hot rice. Serve with shoyu, if desired.
- **Sukiyaki Don:** Cook egg in Sukiyaki (see page 142) and serve on hot rice.

## *Unagi Donburi*
# Rice with Eel Topping

*Yield: 4 to 6 servings*

Rice is prepared with a variety of things in Japan to give it many different flavors. Again, just add a side dish or pickled dish and your bowl meal is complete!

**9 cups hot cooked rice**
**1 (4-ounce) can unagi no kabayaki (cooked eel)**

*Tare (Sauce):*
**1 cup Dashi (see options on pages 14-15)**
**2 teaspoons shoyu**
**2 teaspoons sugar**
**½ teaspoon mirin (sweet rice wine)**

Place rice in donburi (individual bowls); place 2 pieces eel over rice. Combine Tare ingredients; pour ¼ cup over eel. Garnish with peas or minced green onion, if desired.

## *Kai Gohan*
# Clam with Rice

*Yield: 4 to 6 servings*

This dish will become a quick favorite for those who enjoy seafood. Besides, it is easy to prepare.

**2 cups rice**
**2 cups minus 2 tablespoons water**
**2 tablespoons sake (rice wine)**
**1 tablespoon shoyu**
**1½ teaspoons salt**
**1 (6¾-ounce) can clams, drained**

Wash and drain rice. Add remaining ingredients; bring to a boil. Simmer 5 minutes; reduce heat to low and cook additional 15 to 20 minutes or until done. Let stand, covered, 5 minutes before serving.

**Note:** This recipe may be prepared in the rice cooker following the rice cooker manufacturer's directions.

## *Tamago Gohan*
# Shari's Egg and Rice

*Yield: 2 to 4 servings*

Nothing like breaking an egg into a bowl of hot, steaming rice! The egg cooks almost instantly upon contact with the hot rice and a fast snack is ready to be eaten. This was one of the first dishes my daughter, Shari, learned to prepare as a youngster.

**2 large eggs**
**2 tablespoons shoyu**
**¼ cup minced green onion, optional**
**4 cups hot cooked rice**

Combine first 3 ingredients and beat until well-blended. Pour over hot rice; toss gently. Serve immediately.

# Green Peas Rice

*Yield: 4 to 5 servings*

B esides plain rice, the Japanese cook delights in cooking rice with the vegetables of the season—peas, bamboo shoots, mushrooms, carrots, etc.

- **2 cups rice**
- **2½ cups water**
- **2 teaspoons salt**
- **⅓ package frozen peas**

Wash rice and drain. Add water and salt, bring to boil over high heat. Add peas, stir and cover. Bring to a boil again. Reduce heat to simmer and cook for 10 minutes. Turn heat off, leaving cover on, and steam for 10 minutes before serving.

## Variation:

**Bacon Mame Meshi (Bacon Green Peas Rice):** Add 1 strip bacon, minced, to above mixture before cooking.

Note: This recipe may be prepared in the rice cooker following the manufacturer's directions.

## Sake Cha-Zuke
# Salmon with Tea and Rice

*Yield: 4 to 5 servings*

This dish is one of the most popular "comfort foods" for the Japanese.

**Hot green tea**
**Hot cooked rice**
**½ pound salted salmon, cooked and flaked**
**3 tablespoons toasted sesame seeds**

Prepare green tea in teapot. Fill heated donburi with hot rice about two-thirds full; top with salmon flakes and sesame seeds. Pour ½ cup of hot green tea over rice; cover bowl with lid and allow to stand for two minutes before serving.

## Tips:

- To reduce salt in fish, simmer salted salmon in 1 cup boiling water; let stand for 15 minutes. Drain well, then flake before sprinkling over rice.
- Smoked salmon may be substituted for fresh cooked salmon.

# Steamed Glutinous Rice
# with Red Azuki Beans

*Yield: 4 to 6 servings*

*The Japanese associate red and white with happy occasions and so the pretty pale pink and red sekihan (steamed glutinous rice and azuki beans) is often served at birthdays, weddings, and the many seasonal festivals.*

**1 cup dried azuki beans, washed and drained, reserve 5 cups water**
**5 cups water**
**4 cups mochi rice (glutinous rice)**
**1 cup short-grain white rice**
**1 teaspoon salt**
**5 cups azuki water**
**3 tablespoons toasted black sesame seeds**

Wash and rinse the azuki beans; drain and soak in water for 4 hours in saucepan. Bring to a boil; cover and cook over low to medium heat, stirring occasionally to prevent scorching, until beans are tender, about 25 to 35 minutes. Turn off heat; set aside to cool. Drain and reserve cooking liquid, adding additional water to make 5 cups; set aside.

Meanwhile, rinse rice until the water runs clear; drain and place into automatic rice cooker pot. Add salt and azuki water; cover and cook following manufacturer's directions. Let steam 10 to 15 minutes after rice cooker turns off. Stir the cooked rice to ensure that the beans are distributed evenly; sprinkle with sesame seeds and serve.

# Glutinous Rice Cakes (Omochi)

The traditional method of making mochi involves pounding the short-grained Japonica glutinous rice in an intensive ceremonial process called "mochitsuki." Today, commercial mochiko, or glutinous rice flour, puts mochi within the skillset of most home cooks. Still, many families gather for mochi pounding, usually just before the new year.

The customary filling is sweet azuki beans, but contemporary mochi comes with fillings such as chocolate, sweet potato, green tea, peanut butter, and even whole fruit. The treat is enjoyed all year, but is especially important at New Year's and at holiday times such as Boy's or Girl's Day.

Mochi was once served only to the emperor and other nobles, as it was thought to bring good fortune.

# Glutinous Rice Cakes

*Yield: 8 pieces*

*Y*ou can enjoy rice cakes all year 'round by making your own.

> **1 cup mochiko (rice flour)**
> **¼ teaspoon salt**
> **1 tablespoon sugar**
> **½ cup water**
> **Katakuriko (potato starch) or cornstarch**

Stir together in large bowl mochiko, salt and sugar. Stir in ½ cup water to form soft dough; knead lightly, about 30 seconds, on surface dusted with katakuriko. Place dough in greased microwave tube pan. Cover with plastic wrap and microwave on medium-high 10 minutes. Let rest 3 minutes. Turn and cook additional 2 to 3 minutes or until done. Cool. Invert on flat surface sprinkled with katakuriko and cut into serving pieces using plastic knife.

## Variations:

- **An Mochi:** Pinch off walnut-size pieces of mochi. Place 1 tablespoon an in center of mochi circle; pinch edges together to seal; dust with katakuriko.
- **Kinako Mochi:** Prepare mochi as directed. Divide mochi into 8 parts; form into balls and roll in mixture of kinako (soy bean flour) and sugar to serve.
- **Peanut Butter Mochi:** Pinch off walnut-size pieces of mochi. Place 1 tablespoon peanut butter in center of mochi circle; pinch together to seal; dust with katakuriko.
- **Pan-Fried Mochi:** Place mochi in lightly oil sprayed skillet; cook over medium-low heat, turning frequently, until golden brown on both sides. Brush with soy sauce.

# Sushi
# Vinegar-Flavored Rice

The basis of sushi is rice, delicately flavored with sweetened rice vinegar.

The origin of sushi goes as far back as the mid-sixth century to Southeast Asia as a method of preserving fish. Fish was first salt-cured, then packed between layers of steamed rice. The formation of organic acids caused the rice to ferment and flavor the fish, destroying harmful bacteria in the fermentation process.

It was not until the late-seventeenth century that vinegar was added to the cooked rice to give it its characteristic acidic flavor. The addition of vinegar transformed sushi and led to the creation of many different varieties.

There are many varieties of sushi, which may be served as an hors d'oeuvre, as a light lunch, or as one of many dishes on a buffet or at a party.

# Sushi Gohan
# Basic Sushi Rice

*Yield: 9 cups*

**U**se one of these simple sauces to flavor freshly steamed rice to make sushi. The slightly sweet, slightly tangy mixture creates the distinctive flavor of good sushi.

**3 cups rice**
**3 cups water**

***Vinegar Sauce (Awase-zu) Option 1:***
**½ cup rice vinegar**
**2 tablespoons sake (rice wine) or mirin (sweet rice wine)**
**½ cup sugar**
**1 teaspoon salt**

***Vinegar Sauce (Awase-zu) Option 2:***
**3¼ cups rice vinegar**
**¼ cup salt**
**4 to 4½ cups sugar**
**¼ cup mirin (sweet rice wine)**

Wash rice and drain. Add water and let water come to a boil; reduce heat to simmer and cook 5 to 8 minutes or until water level is reduced to level of rice. Cook additional 7 to 8 minutes over low heat. Let steam, covered, 10 minutes before transferring to large bowl or large shallow container.

Combine your choice of Vinegar Sauce ingredients; cook until sugar dissolves; cool. Sprinkle half over hot rice and toss gently. Add more Vinegar Sauce, if desired. Cool quickly. Rice is now ready to make various types of sushi.

*(continued on the next page)*

## Tips:

- Use approximately 1 cup Vinegar Sauce (Awase-zu) to 5 cups cooked rice to make Sushi Rice.
- To toss rice with awase-zu, use cutting strokes sideways across the rice to avoid mashing. DO NOT MIX with circular motions. Cool quickly with a fan.
- Prepared awase-zu may be kept in sealed bottle for later use. The awase-zu may also be used as dressing for tossed greens or raw vegetable slices.

# Bara Sushi
# Tossed Sushi

*Yield: 6 to 8 servings*

Several types of sushi call for a variety of vegetables to be simmered in a flavorful stock. The seasoned vegetables are tossed together with the rice for an easy dish.

**1 recipe Sushi Gohan (see page 41)**

*Vegetables (Gu):*
  **1 medium carrot, slivered**
  **1 medium takenoko (bamboo shoots),**
    **slivered**
  **1 box frozen peas**
  **¼ cup water or Niban Dashi (see**
    **page 15)**
  **½ teaspoon salt**
  **1 teaspoon sugar**
  **2 teaspoons shoyu**
  **2 dried shiitake (mushrooms), softened**
    **in water and slivered**

**1 (4-ounce) can unagi no kabayaki (seasoned eel)**
**Fried egg strips**
**Ajitsuke nori strips**

Combine Gu ingredients; cook 2 to 3 minutes. Drain and cool. Add to Sushi Gohan with unagi; toss gently. Garnish with fried egg strips and nori.

## Tips:

To prepare "Easy Bara Sushi," toss 1 (7½-ounce) can Gomoku-no-tomo with Sushi Gohan and garnish as desired.

# Nigiri Sushi
# Finger Sushi
*Yield: 2½ to 3 dozen*

**N**igiri is the most famous sushi. The hand-molded "finger-shaped" mounds of vinegared rice are topped with slices of seafood. Nigiri was developed in Tokyo as a street finger food.

**4½ cups Sushi Gohan (see page 41)**

**<u>Suggested Toppings:</u>**
**Sashimi**
**Cooked shrimp marinated in Vinegar Sauce for Sushi**
   **Gohan (see page 41)**
**Kamaboko (steamed fish cake)**
**Abalone-like shellfish**
**Cuttlefish**
**Unagi (seasoned eel)**

Shape rice into egg-shaped balls, slightly flattened. Dab a little mustard★ or horseradish paste on top of each rice ball; press on desired topping, cut to fit size of rice ball (about 1 × 1½-inch pieces). Dip in shoyu to eat.

★Mustard: Make paste of 4 teaspoons dry mustard or wasabi with 1½ teaspoons hot water; let stand 5 minutes before using.

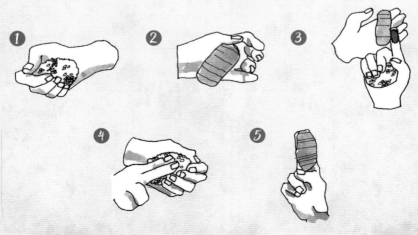

## Nori Maki Sushi/Futomaki
# Sushi Rolled in Seaweed
*Yield: 8 to 10 rolls*

**B**y tradition, norimaki requires layers of various ingredients, each prepared separately before rolling. To serve, using a sharp knife, cut each Futomaki roll into eight pieces. Wipe the knife with a dishtowel dampened with rice vinegar after each cut. Arrange the sushi slices on a large tray and serve with wasabi, gari, and shoyu for dipping.

**1 recipe Sushi Gohan (see page 41)**
**10 sheets sushi nori**

*Filling:*
**1 package (2-ounce) kampyo (dried gourd)**
**4 dried shiitake (mushrooms), softened in water and cut into ½-inch pieces**
**1 small carrot, cut into ½-inch strips**
**10 sprigs watercress, blanched**
**1 (3½-ounce) can unagi (seasoned eel)**

To prepare kampyo: Soak in water 10 to 15 minutes, rub with salt, rinse thoroughly. Cook in 2 to 3 cups of water or dashi until tender, about 20 to 30 minutes. Season with 2 tablespoons shoyu, and 1 tablespoon sugar. Cut into 10- to 11-inch pieces. Cool.

To prepare shiitake and carrot: Cook 5 to 10 minutes or until tender in 1 cup water, 1 tablespoon dried shrimp and 1½ teaspoons salt. Cool.

To roll:
1. Place sheet of nori on sudare (bamboo mat) with edge nearest you even with edge of sudare.
2. Spread Sushi Gohan over nori to a thickness of about ½-inch, leaving ½-inch margin on end farthest from you.

3. In a line 1 inch from edge nearest you, arrange 5 strands kampyo, 1 row each of shiitake, carrot, watercress, and eel, split lengthwise, on the rice.

4. Roll away from you, being careful to hold the vegetables in place with your fingers. When the sudare touches the rice, lift the mat and continue to roll, as you would a jelly roll, until completely rolled.

5. Roll again in the sudare and apply slight pressure to tighten roll.

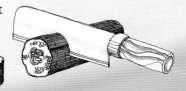

6. To serve, cut each roll into 7 or 8 pieces. Arrange on plate, cut side up.

# Inari Sushi
# Cone Sushi

*Yield: 16 pieces*

**D**eep-fried tofu pouches seasoned delicately with shoyu and sugar makes a delicious wrapping for sushi rice. A variety of vegetables can be mixed in with the sushi rice and if you keep the parcels bite size, they're ideal for picnics and parties.

**1 recipe Sushi Gohan (see page 41)**

## *Vegetables (Gu):*
**2 dried shiitake (mushrooms), softened in water and slivered**
**¹⁄₃ cup finely chopped carrot**
**¹⁄₂ cup finely chopped green beans**
**¹⁄₄ cup minced gobo (burdock root)**
**1 tablespoon dried shrimp**
**¹⁄₂ teaspoon salt**
**¹⁄₂ teaspoon shoyu**
**¹⁄₂ cup broth or Dashi (see options on pages 14-15)**

## *Fried Bean Curd Cornucopia (Aburage):*
**8 triangles aburage**
**2 cups rice water or plain water**
**2 tablespoons dried shrimp**
**1¹⁄₂ cups broth or Dashi (see options on pages 14-15)**
**1 tablespoon shoyu**
**¹⁄₂ teaspoon salt**
**3 tablespoons sugar**

Combine Gu ingredients; cook 10 minutes. Drain and cool. Add to Sushi Gohan and toss gently.

Fried Bean Curd Cornucopia (Aburage):
Cut aburage triangles in half to make two smaller triangles. Carefully remove inner portion from each triangle. Cook in water for 30 minutes or until tender; drain, rinse, drain again. Squeeze out excess liquid.

Combine remaining ingredients and simmer aburage over low heat for 45 to 60 minutes, turning occasionally to season evenly. Drain; cool thoroughly, then stuff with Sushi Gohan mixture.

### Variation:
Sprinkle furikake over rice; toss to mix well and stuff seasoned aburage to make Chirashi Inari Sushi.

### Tips:
- Asian markets have seasoned aburage available for purchase in the refrigerator or freezer section, convenient when hosting a party or in a hurry.
- To open the aburage without breaking them, pull apart gently from the cut end and work toward bottom. When fully open, place finger inside to open corners completely.

# Oshi Sushi
# Molded Sushi

*Yield: 2½ to 3 dozen*

This sushi dates back almost a thousand years and is probably the easiest to make as it utilizes the oshiwaku—a wooden mold—and toppings such as colored shrimp flakes, smoked salmon, or egg strips are placed atop the pressed sushi pieces to serve as a canape-type snack for a party.

**4½ cups Sushi Gohan (see page 41)**

*Condiments:*
    **Oboro-red or green flaked shrimp**
    **Tamagoyaki (fried egg pieces)**
    **Cooked carrots cut in desired shapes**
    **Parsley**
    **Watercress leaves**
    **Kamaboko (steamed fish cake)**
    **Nori**
    **Red ginger slices**

Moisten wooden sushi press with Vinegar Sauce for Sushi Gohan. Top with desired condiments, press through. Repeat with remaining rice and condiments, moistening the press each time.

# *Ika Sushi*
# Cuttlefish Sushi

*Yield: About 2 dozen*

Sushi rice is stuffed into flavorful cooked cuttlefish then sliced crosswise and arranged on an attractive dish for a unique presentation.

**1½ cups Sushi Gohan (see page 41)**

*Gu (Vegetables):*
**2 tablespoons finely slivered carrot**
**4 string beans, finely chopped**
**¼ cup broth or Dashi (see options on pages 14-15)**
**¼ teaspoon salt**

*Ika (Cuttlefish):*
**¼ cup shoyu**
**¼ cup sugar**
**2 tablespoons water or Niban Dashi (see page 15)**
**10 ika (cuttlefish), cleaned and left whole**

Combine all Gu ingredients; simmer 2 to 3 minutes. Drain and cool. Toss with Sushi Gohan.

For ika, combine first 3 ingredients and bring to a boil. Add ika; cook 2 to 3 minutes, turning while cooking. Drain and cool. Stuff cuttlefish cavity with Sushi Gohan. Slice crosswise to serve.

## Temaki Sushi
# Hand-Rolled Sushi

*Yield: 12 to 15 servings*

This is a fun way to enjoy sushi. Temaki means "hand-rolled" and each guest gathers together individual fillings of fish, shellfish, vegetables, and sushi rice.

**Nori (seaweed laver), cut into ½ sheets**
**9 cups Sushi Gohan (see page 41)**
**Wasabi (horseradish paste)**
**1 avocado, skin and seed removed, thin slices**
**1 package kaiware (white radish sprouts)**
**Japanese cucumber, julienned**
**Fresh tuna, salmon, yellowtail (hamachi) strips**
**King crab sticks or imitation crab sticks**
**Spicy Maguro Butsu (Poke; see page 6)**
**Shoyu**
**Spicy mayonnaise**

Arrange all items attractively on platter. Place nori in palm of hand and top with 3 tablespoons of sushi rice; spread rice on nori. Place streak of wasabi along center of rice and lay desired ingredients on top. Wrap nori around filling, starting at lower end of nori and rolling into cone shape. Dip in soy sauce to eat.

## *Menrui*
# Noodle Dishes

**N**oodles are among the most popular foods in Japan. Inexpensive and tasty, they are ideal for a quick lunch or snack. Introduced to Japan in the eighth-century Tang dynasty by Buddhist priests, noodles have developed a national identity of their own.

### *Noodle dishes are available in seven basic types:*
- **Udon**: Round or flat white noodles made from wheat flour
- **Kishimen**: Wide and thick white noodles made from wheat flour indigenous to the Nagoya area and larger than udon
- **Hiyamugi**: Fine white noodles, served cold
- **Somen**: Very fine white noodles, similar to hiyamugi but cottonseed oil or sesame oil is used to moisten the dough
- **Soba**: Grayish noodle made from buckwheat flour
- **Ramen**: Thin, flat, and curly noodle
- **Saimin**: Thin wheat noodle

Noodles are generally served with other ingredients in broth (kakejiru) or with a dipping sauce (tsukejiru) as a one-dish meal.

## *Cooking Noodles:*

Bring 2 or 3 quarts of water to a rolling boil in a large pot. Add noodles gradually, stirring to keep separated. Add tap water 2 or 3 times to prevent boiling over and cook until noodles are tender.

Cook over medium heat following package instructions. It normally takes about:

- 5 to 6 minutes for soba
- 10 to 13 minutes for udon
- 1 to 3 minutes for somen and hiyamugi
- 5 to 8 minutes for ramen

DO NOT OVERCOOK.

Drain in a colander and run cold water over, wash well to remove surface starch. To reheat noodles, place in a handled sieve and plunge into boiling water just until heated through. Garnish and serve in hot soup (kakejiru) or with a dipping sauce (tsukejiru).

## Tip:

Mom's favorite method for cooking dried soba, udon, or somen is called sashimizu, which means to add water while cooking. She believed noodles cooked more evenly using this method. One cup cold water is added to the pot when the water returns to a boil after the noodles have been added. Repeat the process once. Reduce heat and cook 1 to 2 minutes until noodles are al dente.

## Menrui No Kakejiru
# Noodle Broth

*Yield: 4½ cups*

**B**roths for udon and soba noodles are usually made from a fish base and the seasoning is usually milder than most dipping sauces.

**4 cups Ichiban Dashi (see page 14) or Instant Soup Stock (see page 15)**
**¼ cup shoyu**
**3 tablespoons mirin (sweet rice wine)**

Combine ingredients; bring to a boil; cool or continue to simmer until ready to use. Pour over cooked noodles of choice; garnish as desired.

## Tsukejiru
# Dipping Sauces for Noodles

*Yield: 4 to 4½ cups*

**T**he dipping sauces accompanying noodle dishes enhance the flavor of the noodles and are generally more strongly flavored than the broths.

*Tsukejiru #1:*
**3 cups Dashi (see options on pages 14-15)**
**½ cup mirin (sweet rice wine)**
**½ cup shoyu**

*Tsukejiru #2:*
**3 cups Dashi (see options on pages 14-15)**
**2 teaspoons dashi-no-moto granules**
**½ cup mirin (sweet rice wine)**
**⅓ cup shoyu**
**1 tablespoon sugar**
**1 teaspoon salt**

Combine all ingredients and bring to a boil; set aside and cool. Sauce may be refrigerated or frozen for later use. Use as dip for noodles.

# Ramen No Kakejiru
# Saimin Broth

*Yield: 6 to 7 cups*

As a kid, I looked forward to going to my "O-baba's" house in Kaka'ako on weekends so that I could go to the nearby saimin stand for a bowl of hot saimin, garnished with minced green onion and slivers of char siu for lunch.

Broths for saimin or ramen differ from broth for udon or soba as they are made from pork or dried shrimp base, rather than dashi.

**8 cups water**
**¼ cup dried shrimp**
**1 pound pork bones**
**5-inch piece dashi**
   **konbu, wiped and slit**
**½ teaspoon shoyu**
**1 teaspoon salt**

Combine first four ingredients; bring to a boil. Remove konbu. Simmer 1 hour; strain and add seasonings. Pour over cooked ramen; garnish as desired.

## Where Did Saimin Come From?

The exact origin of many local foods is rarely very clear. The word saimin is Chinese—combining "sai" (thin) and "min" (noodles). Many folks, however, believe saimin is more Japanese than Chinese.

Examining the dish itself, saimin noodles are curly and slightly chewy—not exactly Chinese or Japanese. The garnishes are a mixed bag of chopped green onions, strips of fried egg omelet, char siu (Chinese roast pork), kamaboko (Japanese fishcake), Spam®. The soup base, dashi, tastes more Japanese than Chinese, but the classic saimin bowl and ceramic soup spoon are more Chinese. Saimin, of course, is often enjoyed with a side order of "barbecue stick" (teriyaki beef or chicken on a skewer) … very Japanese. Not sure what to make of the small dish of Coleman's mustard and shoyu often used as a condiment.

Perhaps the key element in tracing saimin's genealogy may be that an overwhelming number of saimin restaurants were owned and operated by Japanese, with names like Shiroma's, Shimizu's, Boulevard Saimin, Hamura Saimin, Shiro's Saimin Haven, Washington Saimin, Palace Saimin, Nakai, Zippy's Saimin Lanai, Forty Niner Restaurant, Sam Sato's on Maui, and S&S Brand Saimin (sold at carnivals, fairs and drive-in restaurants throughout Hawai'i), to name a few. Now that's quite a legacy!

# Nabeyaki Udon
## Noodles Cooked in Pot

*Yield: 4 servings*

This dish is often referred to as "pot cooked noodles" because of the heavy earthenware pot used to cook it. It is clearly a "comfort food" filled with lots of tasty, nourishing ingredients.

### Dashi:
  3 cups Dashi (see options on pages 14–15)
  ⅓ cup shoyu
  2 tablespoons mirin (sweet rice wine)
  2 tablespoons sugar

  1 (10-ounce) package cooked udon★
  ½ pound boneless chicken breast, cut into bite-size pieces
  4 shrimp, cleaned and split lengthwise
  ¼ cup takenoko (bamboo shoots), sliced
  8 slices kamaboko (steamed fish cake)
  4 dried shiitake (mushrooms), softened in water
  1 leaf hakusai (won bok or celery cabbage), cut into
    1-inch pieces
  2 stalks green onion, cut into 1½-inch pieces
  4 eggs
  4 pieces Shrimp Tempura (see page 119)

Combine Dashi ingredients in a pot or divide ingredients into four parts and cook in donabe (individual ceramic hot pots); bring to a boil. Add udon and arrange remaining ingredients over udon; cover and bring to boil. Add eggs; turn heat off; cover until eggs are done, about 1 minute. Top with Shrimp Tempura to serve.

### Tip:
Spaghetti noodles may be substituted for udon.

# Somen Salada
# Somen Salad

*Yield: 6 to 8 servings*

Somen was introduced to Japan during the Nara Period from China. As the texture of somen is delicate, it should be cooked "al dente," about 7 minutes.

- 1 head lettuce, shredded
- 1 (8-ounce) package somen (Japanese wheat flour noodles), cooked according to package directions
- 1 cup ham or char siu, julienned
- 1 block kamaboko (steamed fish cake), julienned
- 3 stalks green onion, finely chopped
- Fried egg strips

*Sauce:*
- 2 tablespoons toasted sesame seeds
- 2 tablespoons sugar
- 1 teaspoon salt
- ¼ cup cooking oil
- 3 tablespoons vinegar
- 2 tablespoons shoyu

Arrange lettuce in 9 × 13-inch pan. Top with somen, ham or char siu, kamaboko, green onion, and egg strips.

Mix Sauce ingredients in bottle; cover and shake well. Pour over layered somen salad to serve.

## Hiya Zomen
# Cold Noodles

*Yield: 5 to 6 servings*

Cold somen noodles are often served during the summer and I love serving them in a bowl of cold water with ice cubes, accompanied by a dipping sauce. You'll love the taste of the noodles and the sauce definitely enhances their flavor.

**1 package somen (Japanese wheat flour noodles)**
**1 recipe Tsukejiru or Kakejiru (see page 56)**
**¼ cup minced green onion**
**10 to 12 pieces ajitsuke nori**

Cook somen in 2 quarts boiling water for 3 minutes or as directed on package. Drain, rinse with cold water, and drain again. Chill and serve on ice with Dashi or Tsukejiru. Garnish with green onion and nori.

## Variation:
**Cold Buckwheat Noodles (Zaru Soba):** Substitute soba for somen.

# Sakana No Nitsuke To Somen
# Fish with Somen

*Yield: 4 to 6 servings*

This is a simple and classic dish in which the delicate flavor of the fish simmered in a shoyu-sugar sauce enhances the flavor of the somen.

¼ **cup shoyu**
½ **cup water**
3 **tablespoons sugar**
2 **tablespoons sake (rice wine), optional**
½-**inch piece fresh ginger**
2 **small fish (kūmū, weke), scaled and cleaned**
1 **package somen (Japanese wheat flour noodles), cooked**
   **according to package directions**
½ **cup minced green onion**

Combine first five ingredients and bring to a boil. Place fish in sauce, cover, and cook 10 to 12 minutes. Arrange somen on platter and place cooked fish on noodles. Pour sauce over fish; garnish with green onion to serve. Serve hot or cold.

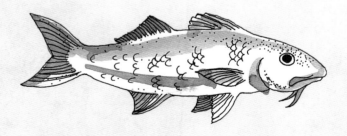

*Menrui*

## *Hiya Ramen*
# Cold Saimin

*Yield: 4 to 6 servings*

**S**aimin is everyone's favorite noodle in Hawai'i! You've just got to have a taste of my dad's cold saimin as it is perfect for lunch on a hot summer day.

**1 (9½-ounce) package dried or raw saimin**

### Condiments (Gu):
**1 small Japanese cucumber, slivered**
**2 cups bean sprouts, blanched**
**1 cup minced green onion**
**1 cup slivered luncheon meat**
**1 cup slivered kamaboko (steamed fish cake)**
**1 tablespoon toasted sesame seeds**

**Fried egg strips**
**Nori strips**

### Dipping Sauce (Tsukejiru):
**½ cup rice vinegar**
**½ cup shoyu**
**½ cup sugar**
**¼ teaspoon sesame seed oil**
**1 package dashi-no-moto**
**Few drops hot sauce, optional**

Cook saimin as directed on package. Rinse, drain, and chill. Arrange noodles in individual serving bowls (on ice, if desired); arrange Gu over noodles.

To prepare Tsukejiru, combine ingredients in a jar; shake thoroughly. Pour over arrangement of noodles and condiments to serve.

# *Yaki Soba*
# Fried Noodles

*Yield: 4 to 6 servings*

*A very popular noodle dish but it isn't made with soba (buckwheat noodle) at all, but with a thin noodle similar to ramen. Meat, fish and vegetables are stir-fried together with the noodles— one of my favorites for lunch.*

   1 tablespoon vegetable oil
   ½ cup boneless chicken or ham, slivered
   1 onion, sliced
   ½ cup carrot, julienned
   ½ cup green onion, cut into 1½-inch lengths
   ½ pound bean sprouts
   ¾ pound fresh fried noodles or yakisoba

*Seasonings:*
   2 teaspoons shoyu
   3 tablespoons chicken broth
   1 teaspoon salt or dashi-no-moto

*Garnish:*
   2 tablespoons toasted sesame seeds
   1 tablespoon beni shoga (red ginger)
   ¼ cup minced green onion or Chinese parsley

Stir-fry chicken in hot oil for 2 minutes. Add vegetables, noodles, and Seasonings; stir-fry 1 minute to heat through. Garnish with sesame seeds, beni shoga, and green onion or Chinese parsley.

# *Aemono, Sunomono, and Tsukemono*
# Mixed Foods, Vinegared Salads, and Pickled Vegetables

**V**egetables play an important role in the diet of the Japanese as many are Buddhists and Buddhism implies vegetarianism.

The Japanese salad has a written history of more than 1,000 years. It is low in calories and delicious—it is no wonder that Aemono, Sunomono, and Tsukemono have served as ideal accompaniments to Japanese cuisine throughout the centuries.

## Aemono (Mixed Foods)

Aemono is a way of dressing foods similar to a Western-style salad. Aemono dishes may be served at the beginning of the meal as well as with the meal.

## Sunomono (Vinegar-Flavored Vegetables)

Vegetables, raw or cooked, and seafoods are marinated in special sauces. In a Japanese meal, they are served to complement the main dishes. Special attention is given to the seasoning and combination so they will enhance and not overpower the featured dishes.

## Tsukemono (Pickled Vegetables)

Japanese pickle dishes are divided into three categories:

- **Shio-zuke**: The vegetables are generously sprinkled with salt and placed under pressure until the liquid is extracted.
- **Su-zuke**: The vegetables are combined with rice vinegar, sugar, and sake (rice wine), and placed in a container under pressure for at least 8 hours.
- **Karashi-zuke**: The vegetables are combined with rice vinegar, shoyu, sugar, and hot mustard; placed in a container under pressure for at least 12 hours.

Tsukemono literally means "soaked" and refers to vegetables that are soaked or preserved in brine or some other type of pickling solution. The vegetable dishes in this category are generally served in individual dishes and accompany the meal.

# AEMONO
## Mixed Foods

*D*ressings for aemono are usually thicker than for sunomono. Base
ingredients may be miso, ground sesame seeds, tofu, egg yolk,
fermented soybeans (natto), or soybean pulp (okara).

## Goma Ae
## Sesame Seed Dressing

*Yield: About ⅓ cup*

¼ cup toasted sesame seeds, crushed
1 tablespoon sugar
2 tablespoons shoyu
3 tablespoons Dashi (see options on pages 14-15)

Combine ingredients; mix well. Mix with cooked vegetables to serve.

## Karashi Ae
## Mustard Dressing

*Yield: About ¼ cup*

1 tablespoon shoyu
2 tablespoons Dashi (see options on pages 14-15)
1 teaspoon Wasabi Paste (see page 95)

Combine ingredients; mix well. Mix with cooked vegetables, pork,
and chicken to serve.

## Shirae
# Tofu Dressing

*Yield: About 1½ cups*

**1 block firm tofu**
**½ cup miso**
**2 tablespoons sugar**
**3 tablespoons toasted sesame seeds**
**1 teaspoon dashi-no-moto granules, optional**

Wrap tofu in double thickness of cheesecloth; squeeze out excess liquid. Place in mixing bowl and mix thoroughly with miso, sugar, dashi-no-moto, and sesame seeds. Toss lightly with cooked vegetables of choice and refrigerate 30 minutes or more before serving.

## Wasabi Ae
# Horseradish Dressing

*Yield: About ¼ cup*

**3 tablespoons shoyu**
**1 teaspoon Wasabi Paste (see page 95)**

Combine ingredients; mix well. Serve with fish and vegetables.

## Miso Mayo Ae
# Miso Mayonnaise Salad Dressing
*Yield: ¾ cup*

**3 tablespoons miso**
**⅓ cup milk**
**⅓ cup mayonnaise**

Combine ingredients and chill. Use as a dressing on a combination of any of the following vegetables: daikon (white radish), lotus root, spinach, watercress, Chinese parsley, chives, won bok, bok choy, endive.

## Peanut Butter Mayo Ae
# Peanut Butter Mayonnaise Dressing
*Yield: ¼ cup*

**¼ cup mayonnaise**
**1 teaspoon creamy peanut butter**

Combine ingredients and serve over cooked vegetables.

# SUNOMONO
## Vinegar-Flavored Vegetables

**S**unomono are made with any combination of raw or cooked vegetables, fruit, seafood, or poultry. They are coated with a thin tangy dressing made with rice vinegar, seaweed dashi, shoyu, and sugar. Sesame seeds, peppers, and other herbs and spices may be added to serve as flavor boosters.

### Goma Zu
## Sesame Seed-Vinegar Dressing

*Yield: About ½ cup*

¼ cup rice vinegar
2 tablespoons shoyu
¼ cup mirin (sweet rice wine)
1½ tablespoons sugar
3 tablespoons toasted sesame seeds, crushed

Combine ingredients; mix well. Use as dressing for cooked or fresh vegetables, cooked shellfish, and fish.

### Amazu
## Sweet Vinegar Sauce

*Yield: ¾ cup*

⅓ cup rice vinegar
⅓ cup sugar
¼ cup mirin (sweet rice wine)
1 teaspoon salt

Combine ingredients in a jar; cover and shake well. Serve with fresh vegetables, cooked shellfish, or fish.

## Ponzu
# Tangy Shoyu Dressing
*Yield: About 1⅓ cup*

### Ponzu A:
*Yields about 1⅓ cups*
- ½ **cup lemon juice or rice vinegar**
- ½ **cup shoyu**
- 2 **tablespoons mirin (sweet rice wine)**
- ¼ **cup Dashi (see options on pages 14-15) or broth, optional**

### Ponzu B:
*Yields about ¾ cup*
- 3 **tablespoons lemon or lime juice**
- 1 **tablespoon orange juice**
- ½ **cup shoyu**
- 2 **tablespoons mirin (sweet rice wine)**

### Ponzu C:
*Yields about 2¼ cups*
- 1 **cup shoyu**
- 1 **cup finely chopped green onions**
- ¼ **cup rice vinegar**
- ¼ **teaspoon hot sauce**
- **Momiji Oroshi (see page 93)**

To prepare your choice of Ponzu, combine ingredients in a jar with cover; shake to mix well. Use as dressing for vegetables, cooked shellfish, fish, beef, or as dip for Shabu Shabu.

## *Oroshi Ae*
# Japanese Radish Dressing

*Yield: 4 servings*

**3 tablespoons rice vinegar**
**1 tablespoon shoyu**
**1 pound cooked shellfish**
**¼ cup grated daikon (Japanese radish)**

Combine first two ingredients; mix well. Marinate shellfish in sauce; drain then combine with grated Japanese radish.

## *Goma Joyu*
# Sesame Seed-Shoyu Dressing

*Yield: ½ cup*

**¼ cup shoyu**
**1½ tablespoons sugar**
**2 tablespoons toasted sesame seeds, crushed**

Combine ingredients; mix well. Use as dressing for cooked vegetables.

## *Sanbaizu*
# Sweet Vinegar-Shoyu Dressing

*Yield: 1 cup*

**¼ cup shoyu**
**3 tablespoons sugar**
**½ cup rice vinegar**
**2 tablespoons mirin (sweet rice wine)**
**½ teaspoon grated fresh ginger, optional**

Combine ingredients; mix well. Use with vegetables.

# Namasu No Moto
# Dad's Basic Vinegar Dressing
*Yield: 2½ cups*

**N**amasu has always been one of our family's favorites and Dad took pride in it being one of his specialties. He added a variety of vegetables such as blanched bean sprouts, canned beet slices, julienne slivers of daikon and carrots, wakame, and more to this basic Namasu Dressing.

**1 cup sugar**
**1 cup rice vinegar**
**1 tablespoon lemon zest**
**Juice of 1 lemon**
**½ teaspoon salt**
**1 tablespoon mirin (sweet rice wine), optional**
**1 tablespoon dried shrimp, rinsed and minced**

Combine ingredients; cover and shake well. Pour over desired vegetables for namasu.

Vegetables generally used for namasu: Cucumber, thinly sliced; seaweed (ogo), cleaned and blanched; radishes, julienned; assorted greens, torn into bite-size pieces; bean sprouts, raw or blanched; beets, sliced; lotus root, cooked and sliced.

*Aemono, Sunomono, and Tsukemono*

## Tori To Yasai No Salada
# Chicken-Vegetable Salad

*Yield: 6 to 8 servings*

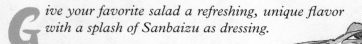

**G**ive your favorite salad a refreshing, unique flavor with a splash of Sanbaizu as dressing.

- 1 **medium head lettuce, broken into bite size pieces**
- 1 **cup celery, cut into thin slices**
- 2 **cups Japanese cucumber, cut into ¼-inch slices**
- 1 **cup carrot, grated**
- 1 **cup cooked chicken, thinly sliced**
- ½ **recipe Sanbaizu (see page 80)**

Combine ingredients. Toss with Sanbaizu (Vinegar Sauce) just before serving.

## Kani No Sunomono
# Crab Salad

*Yield: 4 to 5 servings*

**S**ucculent pieces of crab meat added to fresh, crunchy vegetables make for a very refreshing salad.

- 1 **(6½-ounce) can crab, shredded**
- 1 **medium Japanese cucumber**
- 1 **stalk celery**
- ½ **recipe Sanbaizu (see page 80)**

Cut cucumber in half lengthwise; cut into thin slices. Cut celery into thi n diagonal slices. Combine with crab. Toss gently with Sanbaizu. Chill before serving.

## *Kyuri Sumiso*
# Cucumber with Miso Sauce
*Yield: 6 servings*

The cucumber originated in India in the Himalayas where it has been grown for 3,000 years. This vegetable was first introduced to Japan in the sixth century via China and Korea and gained popularity in the seventeenth century.

- **2 medium Japanese cucumbers**
- **3 tablespoons miso**
- **2 tablespoons sugar**
- **3 tablespoons rice vinegar**
- **2 tablespoons minced green onion**
- **1 can boiled clams, sliced; reserve 1 teaspoon clam juice**
- **2 tablespoons roasted peanuts, ground**

Cut cucumbers in half lengthwise. Seeds may be removed, if desired. Slice cucumbers in thin diagonal slices; set aside. Combine remaining ingredients and mix well. Chill. Just before serving, add cucumbers and toss gently.

# TSUKEMONO
## Pickled Vegetables

### *Bi-ru Tsukemono-No-Moto*
## Beer Pickling Solution

*Yield: About 6 cups*

Quick pickling is preferred by most. A bowl of rice, a cup of hot green tea, and a small side dish of tsukemono constitute the last course in a Japanese meal.

> 1 small box (18 ounces) oatmeal
> 2 cans beer
> 2 cups brown sugar, packed
> ¾ cup salt
> 1 (5-inch) piece dashi konbu

Combine ingredients and add desired vegetables. Let stand 1 to 2 days in refrigerator or at room temperature under 3- to 5-pound weight. Rinse and serve with shoyu.

# Tsukemono-No-Moto
# Mom's Pickling Brine

R emembering Mom's tsukemono—the salty taste, the crisp natural textures, and the characteristic flavor and aroma of fermentation are the qualities of tsukemono that I enjoy most.

## Pickling Brine Solution Option 1:
*Yields 2 cups*
- 1¾ **cups water**
- 1 (5-inch) **piece dashi konbu**
- 1½ to 3 **tablespoons rock salt**
- 1½ **tablespoons sugar**
- ½ **teaspoon shoyu**
- 1½ **teaspoons rice vinegar**
- 1½ **teaspoons sake (rice wine)**

## Pickling Brine Solution Option 2:
*Yields 9 cups*
- 1 **cup brown sugar, packed**
- ⅓ **cup salt**
- ¼ **cup rice vinegar**
- 6 **cups water**
- ¼ **cup shoyu**
- 1½ **cups beer**

**SUGGESTED VEGETABLES: Daikon (Japanese white radish), head cabbage, Japanese cucumbers, eggplants, celery cabbage, Chinese mustard cabbage, daikon green tops, turnip and radish leaves**

Choose one brine solution. Combine ingredients in large container; mix well and add desired vegetables. Let stand 1 to 2 days in refrigerator or at room temperature under 3- to 5-pound weight. Serve with shoyu as a side dish.

### Aka Daikon Amazu
# Pickled Radish

*Yield: 4 servings*

**S**mall red radishes are a relatively recent introduction to Japanese cuisine, however, they are a welcome addition because of their beautiful color. Marinated in a sweetened rice vinegar sauce, they compliment any dish.

> 1 **bunch radishes**
> 2 **teaspoons salt**
> 1 **(6½-ounce) can crab**

**Amazu (Sweet Vinegar Sauce):**
> ⅓ **cup rice vinegar**
> ¼ **cup sake (rice wine)**
> ⅓ **cup sugar**
> 1 **teaspoon salt**

Wash radishes and cut into radish roses (see photo below). Sprinkle with 2 teaspoons salt and let stand 30 minutes. Drain liquid, rinse, and squeeze out excess water using double thickness of cheesecloth. Combine ingredients for Amazu and heat until sugar and salt dissolve. Cool. Mix radish roses with crab; pour Amazu over all; let stand 1 hour. Toss gently before serving.

# *Sanbaizuke*
# Pickled Vegetables
*Yield: 6 cups*

A n easy recipe to prepare. Serve it as a side dish or condiment for a curry dish.

1 (4-ounce) package hanagiri daikon
   (dried white radish)
1 small green papaya, finely sliced
1 medium carrot, finely sliced
1 medium Japanese cucumber,
   finely sliced

*Sanbaizu (Vinegar Sauce):*
   ¾ cup sugar
   1 cup shoyu
   ¼ cup rice vinegar
   1 teaspoon ginger, finely chopped
   1 chili pepper, finely chopped

Soak hanagiri daikon in water for 30 minutes. Drain and squeeze out excess water. Combine ingredients for Sanbaizu and add to vegetables. Store in covered jar in the refrigerator for at least one day before serving.

# *Takuwan*
# Pickled Yellow Radish

*Yield: 1½ pints*

The Japanese radish is Japan's most widely cultivated vegetable. Though there is no record of its introduction to Japan, by the sixth century AD it was already considered to be a noble vegetable and since then it has become deeply incorporated into Japanese cuisine.

¾ **cup vinegar**
1½ **cups sugar**
3 **tablespoons salt**
¼ **teaspoon yellow food coloring**
3 to 4 **medium daikon (Japanese radish), peeled**
1 **small Hawaiian pepper or red pepper flakes to taste**
  **(optional)**

Combine vinegar, sugar, and salt in saucepan. Cook over low heat until sugar and salt dissolve; cool slightly. Add yellow coloring. Slice daikon into ½ × 2-inch strips. Put daikon in a quart jar. Add hot liquid and pepper. Cover jar tightly. Let stand in refrigerator 1 to 2 days before serving.

# Ebi-Makina No Salada
## Shrimp-Chinese Cabbage Salad

*Yield: 4 to 6 servings*

This salad was "tossed" together during one of Mom's creative moments. The shrimp flavor blends in well with the Chinese cabbage—adding minced Maui onions and water chestnuts will kick it up a notch!

**1 pound cooked shrimps, cleaned**
**1 pound Chinese cabbage or won bok (celery cabbage), cooked**

### Seasonings:
**3 tablespoons mayonnaise**
**½ teaspoon salt**
**Dash of salt**
**8 to 16 lettuce leaves**

Wash and cut cabbage into 1-inch pieces. Separate tough, lower ends from tender, leafy portion. Cook stem ends of cabbage in ¼ to ½ cup water for 5 to 6 minutes. Add leafy portion and cook additional 3 to 4 minutes, or until tender. Drain and gently squeeze out excess liquid.

Combine shrimp, cabbage, and seasoning ingredients; mix thoroughly. Chill. Serve in lettuce cups, if desired.

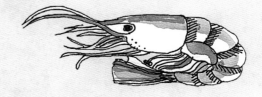

*Aemono, Sunomono, and Tsukemono*

## *Kiri Daikon*
# Dried Radish

*Yield: 1 quart*

The dried radish is obviously not juicy and crunchy like a fresh vegetable but it has an interesting chewy texture and its flavor becomes more intense after soaking in the spicy shoyu base seasonings. Serve as a side dish with rice.

**1 (4-ounce) package hanagiri daikon, soaked and drained**

*Seasonings:*
**¾ cup shoyu**
**Dash chili pepper**
**⅛ teaspoon grated ginger**
**½ cup rice vinegar**
**½ cup sugar**

Mix seasoning ingredients. Pour over daikon and let stand overnight before serving.

# Nasubi No Karashi Zuke
## Mustard Pickled Eggplant

*Yield: 1½ pints*

*T*he mustard is ripened to full flavor in this spicy pickled eggplant, normally served as a side dish.

2 to 3 long eggplants
(3 cups, sliced)
1 tablespoon Hawaiian
rock salt

<u>*Mustard Sauce:*</u>
2 teaspoons mustard
¼ cup shoyu
3 tablespoons sugar
1 tablespoon lemon
juice
1 teaspoon rice
vinegar

Slice eggplant diagonally, about ⅛-inch thick. Sprinkle with salt and let stand for at least 30 minutes. (Eggplant will become limp after salting.) Add a few drops of water to mustard to make a paste; combine with remaining ingredients. Rinse salt from eggplant; squeeze out excess liquid. Add to sauce and mix well. May be served immediately or allowed to stand overnight.

*Aemono, Sunomono, and Tsukemono*

# Minoru & Rose Kamada

*"Don't work just to make money, work to do the best job possible and you will be rewarded."*

— Minoru Kamada

**M**uriel Miura was introduced to the world of cooking at a very early age by her mother, Rose Kamada. "I was cooking rice and helping with basic cooking tasks in the kitchen before I was in the second grade," she recalls. "Mother taught me how to use different methods of Japanese cooking when preparing various types of food."

It was natural, therefore, that Muriel was called upon to help her father, Minoru Kamada, when he acquired a teahouse in 1945. Only about 10 at the time, Muriel would help her father every day after school. Working side-by-side in the kitchen piqued Muriel's interest in cooking. Perhaps more importantly Minoru would stress upon his daughter the values he felt were most important to live by, colored by stories of his very eventful life.

*Celebrating Dad's 91st birthday.*

Even after the teahouse was sold a little more than a year later, the tradition of talking story while preparing food together continued for decades, until Minoru could no longer cook for the family's regular Sunday potluck dinners.

Throughout that time, Minoru's life provided an inexhaustible source of stories. Born in Hawai'i, Minoru's mother, Ritsu, took him to Japan when he was just an infant. His father, Tsurukichi, stayed back in Hawai'i to work. The task of raising Minoru and his four siblings in a remote farming village on Oshima Island, Yamaguchi Prefecture, fell squarely on his mother's shoulders. Even as a child, Minoru worked very hard in the rice fields to support his struggling family.

In 1924, Ritsu somehow managed to purchase Minoru a ticket for passage aboard the *Kasato Maru*, the last ship allowed to sail from Yokohama to Hawai'i. With all of his belongings in a single wicker basket, 16-year-old Minoru endured 14 days of seasickness on the journey to Hawai'i.

Reunited, Minoru and his father soon moved to Kona to work in the coffee fields. Minoru also worked at a local store before moving to Hilo to enroll at the Hilo Boarding School. He studied there for six months and received the equivalent of a third grade English education. He remembered being fed a diet of poi, breadfruit and salted salmon.

Unable to afford to continue his schooling, Minoru went to work at Wainaku Sugar Plantation and cleaned cane haul trucks. He survived primarily on a diet of rice and shoyu in order to save money.

In 1930, Minoru moved to Honolulu and landed a job as a bus boy at the new Royal Hawaiian Hotel. He was promoted to waiter and earned

*My parents, Rose and Minoru Kamada.*

enough to send money to his mother in Japan.

In 1931, Minoru had saved enough money to purchase a truck for $75. He set to work 12 to 14 hours a day selling fish, meat, and vegetables from his truck. Minoru made regular stops at neighborhoods in the Liliha-Kuakini-lower Mānoa areas, ringing a cowbell to announce his arrival.

Minoru married Rose Masako Shimamoto. Muriel was their first child describes Rose as a typical Japanese wife and mother. "She managed to feed us nutritious meals as youngsters; we hardly ever ate out."

Muriel has fond memories of growing up in the Kakaʻako area of Honolulu with her grandparents. "Since my father's family all lived in Japan, my mom's family—aunties, uncles, cousins—played a major role in my life." The houses were all close together in my maternal grandmother's neighborhood, she recalls. "It was like a camp … like a big ʻohana."

Many of Muriel's favorite food memories hearken back to Kakaʻako, like buying luncheon meat sandwiches from a local lunchwagon. "It was just one slice of meat between two slices of white bread (no such thing as whole wheat back then.) That was the best luncheon meat sandwich," she reminisces.

Rice was still cooked over an outdoor fire pit. "It was very old-fashioned rice," she adds. "Then we'd wait for grandfather to come home. He was a fisherman, so we'd use the charcoal in the pit to cook the fish—salted and fried—very simple."

Breakfast at grandma's house was always special—egg and rice. "My mother, who quietly guided me through the years, told me how eggs were always cooked individually when she was a youngster, never scrambled together to feed them all. That way, everyone had their own egg and there was no bickering over who got more. Eaten with hot rice and shoyu…. such a feast!"

Muriel remembers telling her father many times over the years, "Dad, let's put this down." That opportunity passed with him and now it's Muriel who feels it's her responsibility to put down these recipes—and stories—in writing. "This 'stuff' takes so long to learn," she notes. "It's a shame to let it all go down the tube. Perhaps others can gain from what you learned."

*"If you're successful, always remember that you did not do it alone—others put you there."*
— Minoru Kamada

# Sashimi
# Raw Fish

**S**ashimi, most representative of Japan's seafood dishes, is made from the highest quality seasonal fish which is dressed to be served raw. At first bite, the taste should be clean and mild, the texture tender, and the smell fresh like an ocean breeze. The presentation of sashimi is usually regarded as more than just a plate of sliced raw fish. Sashimi might be artistically arranged on a serving plate with fresh herbs and sea vegetables to remind one of a miniature landscape. The merits of good sashimi depend upon freshness, flavor, and texture alone.

### How to Fillet Fish for Sashimi:
1. Scale and wash the whole fish. Cut fish open along belly to remove intestines. Remove fins, head, and hard flaps near head.
2. Starting at the head, cut along back to free the top from the spine and radiating bones. Turn and repeat the process. Bones may be saved for soup or may be cooked with vegetables.
3. To skin the fish, insert knife tip at the tail end of the fillet. Holding firmly onto the skin, pull skin towards you and push the flesh away from you with the side of the knife.

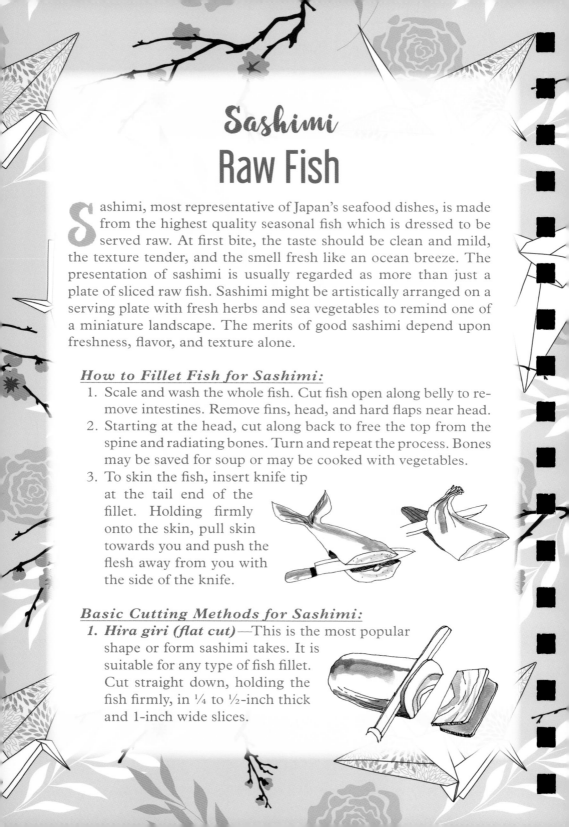

### Basic Cutting Methods for Sashimi:
1. ***Hira giri (flat cut)***—This is the most popular shape or form sashimi takes. It is suitable for any type of fish fillet. Cut straight down, holding the fish firmly, in ¼ to ½-inch thick and 1-inch wide slices.

2. **Kaku giri (cubic cut)**—This method is used more often for tuna. The fish is cut into ½-inch cubes.

3. **Ito zukuri (thread shape)**—This method is often used for squid, though it can be used for any type of small fish. The squid is cut straight down into ¼-inch slices, then cut lengthwise into ¼-inch strips.

4. **Usu zukuri (paper-thin slices)**—The fish is cut at an angle into almost transparent slices.

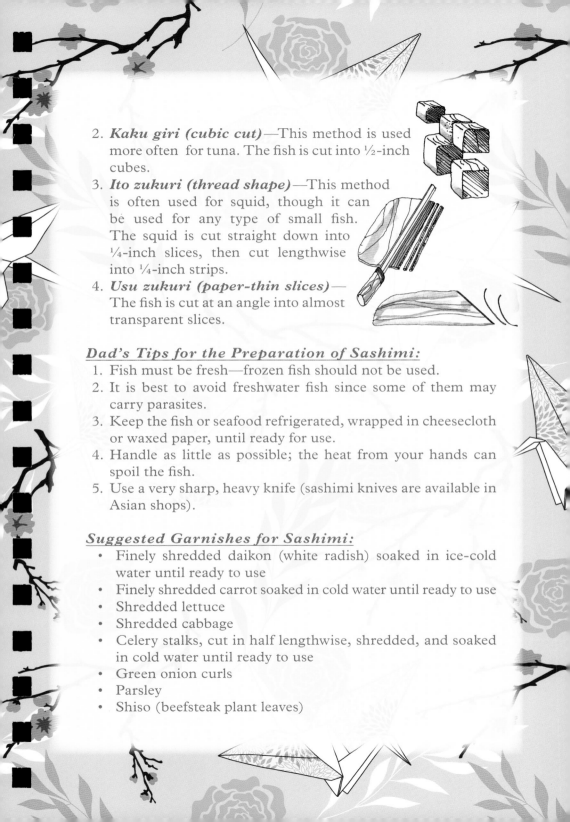

## _Dad's Tips for the Preparation of Sashimi:_

1. Fish must be fresh—frozen fish should not be used.
2. It is best to avoid freshwater fish since some of them may carry parasites.
3. Keep the fish or seafood refrigerated, wrapped in cheesecloth or waxed paper, until ready for use.
4. Handle as little as possible; the heat from your hands can spoil the fish.
5. Use a very sharp, heavy knife (sashimi knives are available in Asian shops).

## _Suggested Garnishes for Sashimi:_

- Finely shredded daikon (white radish) soaked in ice-cold water until ready to use
- Finely shredded carrot soaked in cold water until ready to use
- Shredded lettuce
- Shredded cabbage
- Celery stalks, cut in half lengthwise, shredded, and soaked in cold water until ready to use
- Green onion curls
- Parsley
- Shiso (beefsteak plant leaves)

# Sashimi
## Sliced Raw Fish

*Yield: 4 to 6 servings*

**T**he arrangement of a dish of sashimi is as important as the freshness of the fish. The sashimi can be arranged on one large plate or served in small individual plates. The serving dish is decorated with various garnishes that are also dipped into the shoyu and eaten along with the fish.

**1 pound fresh fillet of 'ahi, porgy, sea bass, striped
  bass, pink or red snapper, ulua, abalone, 'ōpakapaka,
  marlin, or squid
Desired garnishes (see page 89)
Dipping sauces (see pages 93-95)**

To serve sashimi, arrange a bed of greens or garnishes on a platter; attractively arrange one or more varieties of fish on the bed of greens. Place ½ teaspoon mustard or wasabi paste on platter for garnish; refrigerate and serve cold with dipping sauce of your choice.

## Isobe Zukuri
## Nori Wrapped Sashimi

*Yield: 6 to 8 servings*

**N**ori, the most popular seaweed product, is a dried paper-thin sheet of seaweed. It is rich in vegetable protein, vitamins, and minerals and is used for sushi and wrapping rice, fish, meats, vegetables, and other food items. It is also crumbled or shredded for use as a garnish on mixed sushi or noodle dishes.

**1 pound fresh fish fillet
6 sheets sushi nori**

Cut fish fillet into ½- × 7-inch slices. Lay nori on sudare (bamboo mat). Place a long slice of fish along the length of the nori and roll as you would for jelly roll. Cut crosswise in to 1½-inch slices. Serve with desired Sashimi Dip (see pages 93-95).

# Shibi no Tataki
# Yellowfin Tuna Sashimi

*Yield: About 4 to 6 servings*

The thin, singed outer layer of Tataki Sashimi slices makes the presentation of this dish strikingly attractive!

**3 strips (about 1 pound) sashimi-ready 'ahi fillet**
**Salt to taste**
**Ground white pepper**
**1 fresh basil or shiso leaf, broken in pieces**
**4 shallots, finely minced**
**1 medium sweet onion, thinly sliced**

### *Sauce:*
**10 fresh basil leaves, thinly sliced**
**1 (8-ounce) jar Italian dressing**
**1 large ripe tomato, skinned and diced into ½-inch pieces**

Season fish strips with salt, pepper, and basil. Apply minced shallots generously. Singe on all sides in skillet over moderately high heat. This procedure should be watched carefully so as not to brown more than ⅛-inch on all four sides of each fish strip. The center should remain cold and red.

Remove fish from skillet and slice strips into pieces slightly larger than sashimi slices; arrange neatly over bed of sliced onions. Stir to combine Sauce ingredients; pour over fish slices to serve.

### Tip:
Any Sashimi Dip (see pages 93-95) may be used instead of the above Sauce.

# Sashimi Dips

*T*he merits of good sashimi depend upon freshness, flavor, and texture alone, however, careful blending of the right dipping sauce with the sashimi contributes greatly to its flavor.

## Momiji Oroshi
# White Radish and Red Pepper Garnish
*Yield: 6 servings*

**3-inch piece daikon (Japanese white radish), peeled**
**4 dried whole red peppers**
**¼ cup lemon or lime juice**
**¼ cup shoyu**
**¼ cup minced green onion**

Make four openings in the flat side of the daikon. Insert pepper in each opening and set aside 4 hours or overnight.

Grate pepper-stuffed daikon, divide into 6 equal parts. Roll each portion into a ball. Place each portion in individual serving dish; combine with lemon juice and shoyu; garnish with green onion to serve with sashimi.

## Lemon Joyu
# Lemon-Flavored Shoyu
*Yield: 4 to 6 servings*

**¼ cup shoyu**
**1 tablespoon lemon juice**

Combine ingredients and serve as dip for sashimi.

# Chirizu
## Spicy Dip

*Yield: 6 servings*

- 2 tablespoons sake (rice wine)
- ¼ cup grated daikon (Japanese white radish)
- ½ cup minced green onion
- ¼ cup shoyu
- ¼ cup lemon or lime juice
- ⅛ teaspoon hichimi togarashi (seven-pepper spice)

Heat sake in saucepan; ignite with a match and shake pan gently until flame dies out. Pour sake into small dish; cool. Combine sake with remaining ingredients. Pour into individual serving dishes and serve with sashimi.

# Tosa Joyu
## Delicately Flavored Shoyu

*Yield: 6 servings*

- ¼ cup shoyu
- 1 tablespoon sake (rice wine)
- 2 tablespoons katsuobushi (dried fish flakes)

Combine ingredients in saucepan; bring to a boil, stirring constantly. Strain and cool to room temperature. Pour into individual serving dishes and serve with Wasabi Paste (see page 95), if desired. Serve with sashimi.

## Karashi (Wasabi) Joyu
# Mustard-Shoyu

*Yield: 6 servings*

¼ **cup shoyu**
**Mustard or Wasabi Paste (see recipe below)**

Combine shoyu with desired amount of mustard or wasabi paste. Serve as dip for sashimi.

# Mustard or Wasabi Paste

*Yield: 4 to 6 servings*

Wasabi paste is made by grating the root of Wasabia Japonica, Japanese horseradish, which is difficult to grow and expensive. The root loses its sharp, pungent flavor soon after it is grated. As a condiment, real wasabi accentuates the delicate taste of fish. It comes in three forms: Wasabi paste in a squeeze tube, powdered wasabi, and wasabi rhizome (root) which must be grated (expensive and difficult to find at markets).

Most restaurants serve a substitute wasabi condiment made of a mix of horseradish paste, mustard flour, cornstarch, and green food coloring. This type of wasabi has a strong taste that overrules the delicate flavor of fish, however, it is in high demand as it is less expensive.

**1 tablespoon dry mustard or wasabi (horseradish powder)**
½ **teaspoon hot water**

Mix dry mustard or wasabi powder with water until of desired consistency. Set aside 5 minutes before using. Use as garnish or seasoning for sashimi.

# Nimono
# Simmered Foods

Simmered foods are an important part of the Japanese meal. Vegetables, seafood, poultry, and meats are cooked in flavorful seasoned liquids until tender and slightly glazed. There are several variations of seasoning liquids as well as several techniques for simmering the foods. However, dashi (basic stock) is usually the primary seasoning stock. With today's busy lifestyles, convenient instant dashi powder is often substituted for the traditional dashi.

Many of the dishes in this section can be prepared days in advance and refrigerated until ready to serve. Simmered foods are regularly a part of the obento (box lunch).

# Teriyaki Chicken Wings

*Yield: 6 servings*

Chicken wings cooked in flavorful teriyaki sauce can be made a day or two ahead and kept refrigerated until ready to serve.

**2 pounds chicken wings**
**6 to 8 Japanese taro (dasheen)**
**1 stalk green onion, chopped**

*Sauce:*
**²/₃ cup shoyu**
**½ cup brown sugar, packed**
**¼ cup sake (rice wine)**
**½ teaspoon minced fresh ginger**

Cut tips off wings. Peel taro; cut in quarters or halves. Combine Sauce ingredients; heat to dissolve sugar. Add chicken and taro; bring to a boil. Turn heat down to simmer and cook for 30 to 45 minutes; stir occasionally. Add green onion; turn heat off.

# *Umani*
# Vegetables with Chicken

*Yield: 6 to 8 servings*

U mani is prepared by simmering vegetables and chicken in a sauce of basically, shoyu, sugar, dashi, or sometimes, miso. Nimono is a very old form of Japanese cooking which is still preferred by most cooks.

**1 cup boneless chicken, sliced**
**3½ cups Dashi (see options on pages 14-15) or water**
**1 cup gobo (burdock root)★**
**1 strip nishime konbu (dried kelp)★★**
**2 medium carrots, cut into bite-size chunks**
**1 (10-ounce) can takenoko (bamboo shoot)**
**1 konnyaku (tuber root flour cake), cut into bite-size pieces**
**¼ pound Chinese peas, blanched**

### *Seasonings:*
**2¼ teaspoons salt**
**1 tablespoon sugar**
**2 tablespoons shoyu**

Combine first five ingredients and cook 5 to 8 minutes over medium heat. Add remaining vegetables, except Chinese peas; cook additional 10 minutes or until vegetables are done.

Combine Seasoning ingredients and stir to mix thoroughly. Pour over cooked Umani; bring to a boil. Garnish with Chinese peas. Serve hot or cold.

★Gobo—Scrape and cut into ½-inch-diagonal pieces. Soak in water until ready to use.

★★Konbu—Soak in water until softened; wash thoroughly. Tie into knots at 1½-inch intervals; cut between knots.

# Sakana No Nitsuke
# Fish Cooked in Shoyu

*Yield: 6 servings*

Shoyu, which originally came from China, flavors just about all foods in Japanese cooking. Like all other imports to Japan, it was changed to suit Japanese tastes, to become a lighter seasoning than the soy sauce from China.

- ⅓ **cup shoyu**
- ½ **cup water**
- 1 **tablespoon sake (rice wine) or mirin (sweet rice wine)**
- 3 **tablespoons sugar**
- ½**-inch piece fresh ginger, crushed**
- 6 **(1½ to 2-pound size) whole fish (red snapper, 'ōpakapaka), or 6 pieces fish fillet**

### *Seasonings:*
**Minced green onion or cilantro, optional**

Combine first 5 ingredients in large saucepan and bring to a boil. Place fish in single layer in sauce, cover, and simmer 8 to 12 minutes or until fish is cooked. Do not overcook.

Serve spoonful of sauce over fish and garnish with green onion or cilantro, if desired.

# Nishime
# Cooked Vegetables

*Yield: 4 to 6 servings*

This tasty vegetable dish is one of the traditional foods for the Japanese New Year. Nishime is often also part of the popular obento.

¼ cup iriko (dried fish)
1 aburage (fried bean curd), sliced
3½ cups water or Dashi (see options on pages 14-15)
1 cup gobo (burdock root), cut into ½-inch diagonal pieces, soaked in 1 cup water with 1 teaspoon vinegar for 10 minutes
1 strip nishime konbu (dried kelp), soaked, knotted, and cut between knots
2 medium carrots, cut into ½-inch diagonal pieces
1 (10-ounce) can takenoko (bamboo shoot), cut into ½-inch diagonal pieces
1 konnyaku (tuber root flour cake), cut into bite-size pieces
12 small dasheen (Japanese taro), peeled, soaked in water, and cut into large chunks

### Seasonings:
¼ cup shoyu
3 tablespoons sugar
1½ teaspoons salt

Combine first five ingredients; cook 15 to 20 minutes or until konbu is tender. Add remaining ingredients; cook 5 minutes or until vegetables are done. Add Seasoning ingredients; toss gently. Serve hot or cold.

# Tori No Kayaku Nabe
## Mom's Chicken Macaroni

*Yield: 6 to 8 servings*

This dish was Mom's specialty and served as "comfort food" for our family when we were young. It's a dish concocted by my grandmother.

**3 cups water**
**3 tablespoons shoyu**
**2 tablespoons sugar**
**1 tablespoon salt**
**1½ pounds boneless chicken, chopped into 1½-inch pieces**
**1 medium carrot, cut into 1½-inch slants**
**1½ cups bamboo shoot, sliced into ½-inch slices**
**½ pound string beans, cut into 1½-inch pieces**
**4 cups cooked macaroni**

Combine first five ingredients and simmer 10 minutes. Add carrots and bamboo shoot; simmer 5 minutes. Add string beans and macaroni; cook additional 10 minutes.

# Buta No Kayakunabe
## Pork and Vegetables

*Yield: 6 servings*

*P*ork gives any dish a light, delicate flavor and its flavor does not dominate the dish ... it enhances the natural flavor of the other ingredients.

**4 dried shiitake (mushrooms), cut into fourths**
**½ pound pork, sliced into ¼-inch strips**
**1 tablespoon vegetable oil**
**½ cup water**
**1 cup carrot, peeled and cut into ¼-inch slants**
**1½ cups burdock root, peeled and cut into ¼-inch slants**
**1½ cups bamboo shoot, cut into ¼-inch slants**
**1 medium round onion, sliced**
**1 cup green onion, cut into ½-inch lengths**

### *Seasonings:*
**½ teaspoon salt**
**1 teaspoon shoyu**

Soak dried mushrooms in 1 cup water for 30 minutes. Squeeze water from mushrooms; remove stems and cut into fourths. Stir-fry pork in hot oil for 1 minute. Add water, carrots, and burdock root, simmer for 10 minutes. Add round onion, mushrooms, and seasonings; simmer for 5 minutes. Stir in green onion just before serving.

# Kabocha No Fukumeni
## Simmered Pumpkin

*Yield: 4 to 6 servings*

**S**immered in a delicate sauce which enhances its fresh, natural flavor, this dish can be served either hot or cold. If your past experience with pumpkin has been limited to pies, try this new taste treat.

1½ **pounds kabocha (pumpkin)**
2½ **cups Dashi (see options on pages 14-15)**
2 **tablespoon mirin (sweet rice wine)**
⅓ **cup sugar**
1 **teaspoon salt**
2 **teaspoons shoyu**

Cut kabocha in half lengthwise, then cut into wedges along the grooves, about 2-inches thick. Remove seeds and peel skin at 1-inch intervals, leaving strips of green.

Combine dashi with seasonings in a saucepan; bring to a boil; add kabocha. Cover and cook on medium-high heat and bring to a boil. Reduce heat and simmer for 10 to 15 minutes, or until kabocha is cooked. Turn heat off and let kabocha stand in sauce until ready to serve.

# Eda Mame Buta Ni
## Pork with Green Beans

*Yield: 4 servings*

Seasoned simply with sugar, sake and shoyu, this dish of green beans can be served either as a main course or side dish in a Japanese meal. Don't forget the hot green tea, rice, and pickled veggie.

½ **pound lean pork, sliced thin**
1 **clove garlic, minced**
1 **tablespoon oil**
1 **medium onion, sliced**
½ **pound string beans, cut in 2-inch lengths**

### *Seasonings:*
1 **tablespoon sugar**
2 **tablespoons sake (rice wine)**
2 **tablespoons shoyu**
½ **cup water**

Sauté pork and garlic in hot oil for 1 minute. Add onion, string beans and combined seasoning ingredients. Cook 3 to 5 minutes over medium flame. Serve hot with rice.

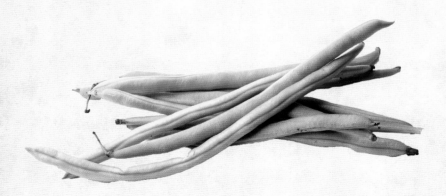

# Mame Sato Ae
## Sweet Lima Beans

*Yield: 6 servings*

**M**om loved her dish of sweetened lima beans with a bowl of tea and rice for a light lunch along with a piece of fish and some tsukemono. She substituted canned kidney beans for lima beans on occasion for variety.

1½ **cups dried**
   **lima beans**
4½ **cups water**
¾ **cup sugar**
½ **teaspoon salt**

Soak beans in water to cover overnight; drain. Combine soaked beans with water in saucepan and bring to a boil. Reduce heat and simmer over low heat 1 to 2 hours or until beans are soft. Add sugar and salt; cook additional 10 minutes, stirring occasionally. Cover and let stand 1 hour. Pour out excess liquid, if any, into another saucepan; cook until liquid is reduced and return to beans. Bring to a boil once more and remove from heat. Serve as a side dish.

## Mushimono
# Steamed Foods

**S**avory soup-custards, filled wheat buns and glutinous rice are among favorite foods for steaming in Japanese cuisine. Steaming is a popular and healthy cooking method utilized for centuries because it is fast and economical. It also preserves the natural flavors, colors, and nutrients of the foods. Steamed foods are also self-basting, whereby moisture is retained.

## Chawan Mushi
# Steamed Custard
*Yield: 6 servings*

B e a creative cook and prepare delicious chawan mushi that includes many little bits of tasty treasures such as chicken, fish, vegetables, and mushrooms hidden in the decorative cups of hot egg custard.

### Shrimp Stock:
¼ cup dried shrimp
5 cups water
1 teaspoon shoyu
½ teaspoon salt
1 teaspoon sugar

3 dried shiitake (mushrooms), soaked in warm water
½ cup water
1 teaspoon shoyu
¼ teaspoon salt

¼ pound fresh shrimp
1 bamboo shoot, julienned
⅛ pound Chinese peas
4 eggs

To make Shrimp Stock, simmer dried shrimp in water for 30 minutes. Cool, season with shoyu, salt, and sugar.

Cook mushrooms in water, shoyu, and salt until tender. Cool; sliver mushrooms. Add mushroom stock to shrimp stock.

Cook fresh shrimp in salted water for 4 to 5 minutes. Arrange shrimp, mushrooms, bamboo shoot, and peas in individual chawan mushi bowls with covers. Beat eggs, add 4 cups cooled stock. Pour into individual bowls. Cover and steam for 20 to 30 minutes, or until custard is set. Serve hot.

# Mushi Zakana
# Poached Fish

*Yield: 2 servings*

t is always a delight to have poached fresh fish drizzled with a light shoyu-oil sauce served on a decorative platter. Garnish with garden fresh minced green onion for a touch of color.

**1 (2½- to 3-pound) mullet, moi, weke or catfish**
**2 slices fresh ginger**
**Boiling water**

*Sauce:*
**2 tablespoons shoyu**
**1½ tablespoons vegetable oil**
**2 tablespoons minced green onion**

Scale and clean fish. Place fish and ginger in pot of boiling water to cover. Cover with tight fitting lid; let stand 30 minutes or until done. Place fish on platter.

Combine Sauce ingredients; pour over fish to serve. Garnish with green onion curls, if desired.

## Sakana No Mushimono
# Steamed Fish

*Yield: 2 to 4 servings*

For a touch of elegance, steam a whole fish topped with Japanese vegetables and lemon slices on an oval heat-resistant platter. This delicately flavored dish will certainly impress your guests.

1 (1½- to 2-pound) mullet, kūmū, or catfish, scaled and
  cleaned
½ teaspoon salt
4 slices round onion
¼ cup takenoko (bamboo shoot), slivered
½ cup green onion, cut in 1-inch pieces
5 slices lemon
2 dried shiitake (mushrooms), softened in water and
  slivered

### Sauce:
2 tablespoons shoyu
¼ teaspoon grated fresh ginger

Salt fish; place on heat-resistant platter and arrange round onion, takenoko, green onion, lemon, and shiitake on fish. Cover and steam 20 to 25 minutes, or until done. Serve with ginger–shoyu sauce.

### Tip:
To soften dried mushrooms, soak in hot or warm water 15 to 30 minutes. Squeeze out excess liquid; prepare as directed in recipe.

## *Wakadori No Karei Mushi*
# Steamed Curried Chicken

*Yield: 2 to 4 servings*

Chicken returned to the Japanese table in the mid-nineteenth century, after a 1,200-year absence and quickly gained popularity. In Japan today chicken is eaten more than any other meat. It is popular for its milder taste and its ability to partner well with other ingredients and flavors, like curry.

**4 chicken thighs**
**2 teaspoons salt**
**1 tablespoon curry powder**
**1 small round onion, cut in wedges**

Salt chicken and sprinkle with curry. Arrange alternately with onions on heat-resistant dish. Steam 30 to 45 minutes, or until done.

## Siu Mai
# Steamed Pork Dumplings

*Yield: 2 to 2½ dozen pieces*

**S**team-cooking is a gentle way of applying heat to an ingredient. It is a suitable method of cooking delicately flavored items such as these popular pork dumplings which are often served as appetizers or sides.

### Filling:
- ½ **pound lean ground pork**
- 1 **egg, slightly beaten**
- ½ **teaspoon shoyu**
- ¼ **teaspoon sesame seed oil**
- ½ **teaspoon salt**
- 1 **teaspoon sake (rice wine)**
- ¼ **cup minced green onion**
- 2 **tablespoons minced water chestnuts**

**Wonton wrappers**

Combine Filling ingredients and mix well. Fill center of wonton wrappers with 1 tablespoon filling. Moisten edges; gather wrapper around filling and pinch lightly to form packet, leaving top open. Steam 20 to 25 minutes. Serve hot or cold.

# Remembering Sunday Suppers

For as long as I can remember, Sunday was family day for catching up with the cousins, sharing our lives at the table. It was a tradition that traveled from my grandmother's house to my parents'.

Every Sunday my mother took us to her mother's house in Kaka'ako, on Halekauwila Street near Ward Avenue. My grandmother had nine children and most showed up for Sunday suppers, with their spouses and all the grandkids. I was the oldest.

It was potluck with typical country-style Japanese foods such as nishime, shoyu chicken, maze gohan, and salad. My mother's oldest brother's wife did most of the cooking. There was a fireplace outside specifically to cook rice in a heavy metal rice pot (kama) with a lid. I loved hanging around there, waiting for the rice to get crispy to make musubi.

We always had sashimi thanks to my grandfather, who was a fisherman. He worked out of Kewalo Basin and went out to the deep water for 'ahi. (My grandmother, thanks to Grandpa's vocation, had her own avocation—bootlegging. The men needed a bit of booze to keep them warm out on the ocean. So during the Prohibition years she sometimes brewed sake from rice, just enough to keep the fishermen going.)

Most of Grandpa's catch was sold but he brought the "scraps" home for us. We loved 'ahi belly. My aunt would cook the heads with ginger and shoyu in a huge pot. This was nimono, a traditional Japanese technique of stewing or long-simmering. So delicious. I also remember the huge fish collars that were simply salted and broiled to perfection.

Our family also had beach cookouts on the Wai'anae Coast, where my uncle and aunt lived. One Sunday each month we would pile into the car for the three-hour drive (no freeway in those days), crowded in with insulated boxes full of musubi, namasu, and meat for the hibachi.

These larger family gatherings tapered off as our generation grew up and left home, but Sunday suppers continued at my parents' house, with my brother and me bringing our families every week.

*My mother and father at one of our Sunday suppers.*

My father and I did most of the cooking for our group of nine. Our planning was very informal—"Last week we had meat, so this week let's have fish." Some of our favorites were shrimp and vegetable tempura, broiled sea bream with mayonnaise, namasu, sukiyaki, yakiniku, and more.

Just as Sunday suppers at my grandmother's always included sashimi, so did our dinners. Every Saturday morning my dad would go to Chinatown to buy fresh fish. He was the cook in our family, the one who taught me how to pull a chicken apart and how to clean and cook fish. By the time I was six or seven years old I knew how to do all those things.

As our own children grew up and left home, Sunday suppers became just the six of us—my parents, my brother and me, and our spouses. We continued the tradition until about 2000, when my parents were too frail.

If my daughter and her family lived nearby, Sunday suppers might have continued for another generation. Instead, I look to my cookbooks—beginning with *Cook Japanese* in 1974, as my way of passing on the homestyle dishes of my childhood to my grandchildren. While this book is rooted in the Japanese culinary arts that I have explored all of my professional life, the specific dishes clearly speak of Hawai'i and of home, of Sunday suppers, and the spirit of family.

# *Agemono*
# Fried Foods

In the mid-sixteenth century Japan had its initial contact with the West. Portuguese missionaries introduced their native method for deep-frying seafood. The Japanese adopted this new method for deep-frying and refined their techniques, elevating deep-frying to a fine art.

Undoubtedly, the most popular deep-fried food in the Japanese diet is tempura. Tempura is an example of the batter-frying technique called koromo age, in which piping hot pieces of batter-coated seafood and vegetables are lifted from hot oil and served immediately.

# *Tempura*
# Japan's Most Popular Fried Food

The original tempura dish was introduced to Japan by European missionaries more than 300 years ago. To prepare good tempura, there are some basics that you should be aware of:

1. Use good quality oil
2. Use fresh ingredients
3. Use correct oil temperatures:
   - 300 to 365°F for vegetables
   - 350 to 375°F for seafood, beef, etc.

My dad taught me that the most important ingredient for good tempura is the oil. Various types of oils are used—mineral, vegetable, animal—depending on personal preferences, but vegetable oil is most common. Some tempura specialty restaurants in Japan blend their own oils. A popular combination is soybean and sunflower. Following are suggestions for other blends of good quality tempura oil:

- 70% peanut oil, 30% sesame seed oil
- 85% cottonseed oil, 10% olive oil, 5% sesame seed oil
- 75% peanut oil, 20% sesame seed oil, 5% olive oil
- Vegetable oil (canola, corn, vegetable)

For that "perfect" tempura, here are tips from Japanese chefs:

1. Use ice-cold water.
2. Keep batter chilled.
3. Coat food thinly with batter.
4. Do not overmix batter; leave lumps.
5. Prepare small amounts of batter at a time.
6. Cook a small quantity at a time.
7. Serve hot.
8. Do not overcook.

Though there are hundreds of recipes for tempura, only my famiy's basic one is featured in this section. Tempura ingredients may be added or deleted to suit individual tastes.

# *Koromo*
# Tempura Batter

*Yield: About 2 cups batter*

*A*lways use ice-cold water, mix small quantities of batter just before use and do not over mix the batter—a few lumps will not harm the batter.

**½ cup flour**
**½ cup cornstarch**
**1 egg**
**½ cup cold water**

Sift dry ingredients together; beat egg and water together. Add liquid, all at once, to dry ingredients, mixing only until dry ingredients are moistened; batter will be lumpy. Dip seafood and vegetables into batter; deep-fry in oil heated to 365 to 375°F until delicate brown. Drain and serve hot with Tempura Sauce (see page 120).

For Lacy Tempura:
Remove ½ cup batter and add 2 tablespoons water for thin lacy batter. The remaining portion is the thick dipping batter.

Dip fingers into think batter and sprinkle over hot oil, heated to 365 to 375°F. Repeat several times until lacy network is formed. Dip prepared seafood or vegetable into thick batter and place on lacy network. When tempura is delicately brown, break network of batter to separate individual tempura; turn and fry additional minute. Drain and serve with Tempura Sauce while hot.

Some suggested ingredients for tempura are:
- Fish fillets
- Shrimps
- Asparagus spears
- Burdock root
- Sweet potato, ¼-inch slices
- Lotus root, ¼-inch slices
- Eggplant, ¼-inch slices
- Ginkgo nuts on skewers
- Bell pepper, wedged
- Round onion, sliced
- Bamboo shoot, sliced

# Tempura No Tsukejiru
## Tempura Sauce

*Yield: 4 servings*

S erve the warm sauce in small bowls. Tempura tastes best when lightly dipped into the sauce, then immediately eaten.

**2 cups water**
**5-inch piece dashi konbu**
**½ cup katsuobushi (dried fish flakes)**
**2 teaspoons shoyu**
**½ teaspoon salt**
**½ teaspoon sugar**
**½ cup grated daikon (Japanese radish)**
**1 tablespoon minced green onion**

Bring water to boil. Add konbu and cook 10 minutes. Add katsuobushi and simmer 3 minutes. Strain. Return liquid to pot. Add shoyu, salt, and sugar. Bring to boil. Cool. Just before serving, add daikon and green onion.

# Karei Age
# Curried Seafood Tempura

*Yield: 4 to 5 servings*

For a change, add curry powder to the batter mix for a touch of spice in your fried seafood dish.

**1 cup sifted flour**
**1 teaspoon curry powder**
**½ teaspoon salt**
**1 egg, beaten**
**1 cup cold water**
**1 tablespoon minced green onion**

**½ pound jumbo shrimp**
**½ pound scallops**
**½ pound fish fillets ('ahi, mahimahi, etc.)**

**Vegetable oil for deep-frying**

Sift dry ingredients together. Combine egg and water. Add to dry ingredients along with green onions and mix well.

Wash and shell shrimp leaving the tails. Split shrimp down the center of the back and open flat. Remove black vein. Place shrimp cut-side down, and score to prevent curling. Cut fish fillets in 2 × 2½-inch sticks. Cut large scallops in half.

Dip seafood in batter and fry in oil heated to 365°F until lightly browned. Drain on absorbent paper and serve hot with shoyu or Tempura Sauce (see page 120).

# Iga Age
## "Thorny" Tempura

*Yield: 2 dozen*

Fishcake, shrimp, scallops, or fish are rolled in broken pieces of somen noodles then fried, forming an attractive "thorny" dish which can be served as an appetizer or side dish.

**½ pound raw seasoned fish cake, or 1 pound shrimp, cleaned**
**½ cup flour**

### *Batter:*
**1 egg, slightly beaten**
**½ cup water**
**½ cup flour**
**½ cup cornstarch**

**4 ounces somen (Japanese wheat flour noodles), broken into ¾-inch pieces**
**1 quart canola oil for frying**

Form fishcake into walnut-sized balls. Dredge fishcake or shrimp in flour and set aside. Add egg to water and beat to combine; add to flour and cornstarch mixture and stir until ingredients are blended together.

Dip fishcake balls or shrimp into batter; roll in somen. Deep-fry in oil heated to 365°F, until golden brown. Drain on absorbent paper and serve hot.

### Variation:
Substitute chicken, fish fillet, or scallops for fish cake or shrimp.

# Ebi No Kaki-Age
## Shrimp Fritters

*Yield: 18 to 24 fritters*

**W**hat can be easier to prepare than these fritters? Mix all the ingredients in a bowl, form the dough into patties, and fry them in hot oil for a minute and they're ready to serve!

- ¾ **cup flour**
- ½ **teaspoon salt**
- 2 **teaspoons sugar**
- 1 **egg**
- ¼ **cup water**
- ½ **cup minced fresh shrimp**
- ¼ **cup minced green onion**
- 1 **quart oil for frying**

Combine dry ingredients. Add egg to water and beat until foamy. Mix into dry ingredients, stirring only to moisten dry ingredients. Add shrimp and green onion. Form patties. Drop by spoonfuls into oil heated to 365°F. Fry 1 minute or until delicately brown. Drain on absorbent paper. Serve with meal or as pūpū while hot.

# Kamaboko Tempura
## Fish Cake Fritters

*Yield: 18 to 24 fritters*

*P*leasantly chewy pieces of fish cake are mixed with batter and fried. Add them to noodles dishes and salads or just enjoy them as wonderful snacks.

³⁄₄ **cup flour**
¹⁄₂ **teaspoon salt**
2 **teaspoons sugar**
1 **egg**
¹⁄₄ **cup water**
¹⁄₂ **cup minced kamaboko (steamed fish cake)**
¹⁄₄ **cup minced green onion**
**Vegetable oil, for deep-frying**

Combine dry ingredients. Add egg to water and beat until foamy. Mix into dry ingredients, stirring only to moisten dry ingredients. Add kamaboko and green onion. Drop by teaspoonfuls into oil heated to 365°F. Fry 1 minute or until delicately brown. Serve with meal or as pūpū while hot.

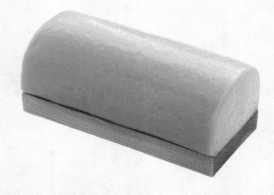

# Ebi No Harusame Age
## Shrimp–Long Rice Fritters

*Yield: 4 to 6 servings*

For an awesome presentation of shrimp, coat both sides with snipped pieces of harusame (bean thread noodles). When deep-fried, the noodles expand, forming an attractive puffed-noodle coating. Your guests will be impressed!

**1 pound fresh shrimp, cleaned**
**½ teaspoon salt**
**½ cup cornstarch**
**2 eggs, slightly beaten**
**1 bundle long rice (bean thread), cut into 1-inch pieces**
**1 quart canola oil for frying**

Sprinkle shrimp with salt. Dredge in cornstarch, then dip into egg. Coat both sides of shrimp with long rice. Deep-fry in oil heated to 375°F for 1 minute, or until delicately browned. Drain on absorbent paper and serve hot with Tempura Sauce (see page 120).

# Kaki-Age
## Fried Oysters

*Yield: 4 to 6 servings*

Oysters are a naturally flavorful delicacy and all it takes is a simple preparation to make them 'onolicious.

**1 pound fresh or frozen oysters, thawed and drained**
**1 egg, slightly beaten**
**2 cups bread or corn flake crumbs**
**1 quart vegetable oil for frying**

Dip oysters in egg. Dredge in bread or corn flake crumbs. Fry until golden brown in oil heated to 365°F. Drain on absorbent paper. Serve with purchased Chili Sauce or Tempura Sauce (see page 120).

# Iso Age
# Fried Seaweed Roll

*Yield: 32 rolls*

*D*eveloping a taste for seaweed and learning how to use it as a food is wel- worth the effort. Nori, the most popular, is used in this recipe as a wrap for salmon filling. This seaweed roll makes an excellent appetizer or may be added to the bento box.

> 1 (No. 1) can sockeye salmon, boned
> ½ cup round onion, minced
> ½ cup green onion, finely chopped
> 2 eggs
> ¼ teaspoon salt
>
> 6 sheets nori (seaweed)
> 1 quart vegetable oil for frying

Combine the first five ingredients and mix well. Cut each sheet of nori into fourths and spread one to two teaspoons of salmon mixture on each piece of nori, leaving ½-inch margin on end farthest from you. Roll away from you, as you would a jelly roll, and pinch the ends slightly to seal. Deep-fry in oil heated to 365°F for 1 to 2 minutes. Drain on absorbent paper and serve hot.

# Ebi No Karei Age
## Curried Shrimp
*Yield: 4 servings*

**U**se top-quality oil for frying. The oil must be light and have a neutral flavor to allow natural food flavors to be highlighted.

**1 pound fresh or frozen shrimp, cleaned**
**1 egg, slightly beaten**
**1 cup corn flake crumbs**
**1 quart vegetable oil for frying**

*Marinade:*
**1 tablespoon shoyu**
**1 tablespoon sugar**
**1 teaspoon salt**
**2 teaspoons curry powder**
**2 tablespoons cornstarch**
**1 tablespoon sake (rice wine)**

Butterfly shrimp. Combine Marinade ingredients and marinate shrimp 20 to 30 minutes. Dip in beaten egg and dredge in corn flake crumbs.

Deep-fry in oil heated to 365°F until golden brown. Drain on absorbent paper. Serve hot.

# Mahimahi No Karei Age
## Curried Mahimahi

*Yield: 4 servings*

**M**ahimahi marinated in a curry sauce, crusted with corn flakes then fried to a golden brown will surely become one of your favorite fish recipes. Other white fish fillets may be substituted for mahimahi. For a touch of Hawai'i, some mango chutney on the side will go well with the curried fish.

    1 pound mahimahi fillet
    1 egg, beaten
    1 cup corn flake crumbs
    1 quart canola oil for frying

*Marinade:*
    1 tablespoon sugar
    1 teaspoon salt
    1 tablespoon sake (rice wine)
    2 teaspoons curry powder
    2 tablespoons cornstarch
    1 tablespoon shoyu

Cut fish into serving pieces; score. Combine Marinade ingredients and marinate fish 30 minutes. Dip fish into egg and dredge in corn flake crumbs. Deep-fry in oil heated to 365°F until golden brown, about 3 to 4 minutes on each side. Drain on absorbent paper. Serve hot.

# *Tonkatsu*
# Pork Cutlet
*Yield: 3 to 4 servings*

S ome cooks rely on instinct and familiar signs to gauge oil temperatures for deep-frying. It may help novice cooks to use a deep-fat thermometer, or dip a pair of wooden cooking chopsticks into the hot oil; bubbling activity around the chopsticks indicates the oil has reached about 360°F. You can test the oil by frying a small cube of bread. The bread cube will rise in a few seconds if the oil is in the 350°F range.

1 pound lean pork, cut into ½-inch-thick slices
½ teaspoon salt
1 egg, slightly beaten
1½ cups corn flake crumbs, dry bread crumbs,
  or panko
1 quart canola oil for frying

### *Sauce:*
½ cup catsup
3 tablespoons Worcestershire sauce
Dash of pepper

Salt pork and dip in beaten egg. Dredge in panko, corn flake, or dry bread crumbs, and fry in oil heated to 365°F for 2 to 3 minutes or until golden brown. Drain on absorbent paper.

Mix Sauce ingredients and blend thoroughly. Spoon sauce over cutlets.

## Variation:
**Gyuniku Katsu (Beef Cutlet):** Substitute top sirloin or any tender cut of beef for pork.

## Kara Age
# Fried Chicken-Japanese Style

*Yield: 4 to 6 servings*

This is the Japanese version of fried chicken. It is marinated in a shoyu-base sauce, then dredged in starch before frying. It is a popular chicken dish served at parties.

**1 fryer chicken, cut into bite-size pieces**

**Marinade:**
**½ cup shoyu**
**¼ cup sugar**
**1 clove garlic, crushed**
**½ cup sake (rice wine) or mirin (sweet rice wine)**
**1 piece fresh ginger, crushed**

**Cornstarch or katakuriko (potato starch)**
**Vegetable oil for frying**

Combine Marinade ingredients; mix thoroughly. Marinate chicken for 1 hour. Drain; dredge in cornstarch or potato starch and deep-fry in oil heated to 365°F. until golden brown. Drain on absorbent paper. If desired, heat Marinade and pour over chicken to serve.

# *Torikatsu*
# Chicken Cutlet

*Yield: 4 to 6 servings*

C hicken thighs may be substituted for breasts in this recipe but I prefer the even cooking resulting from the breast cutlets.

**2 pounds boneless chicken breast, skin removed**
**½ cup flour**
**2 egg, beaten**
**2 cups panko (bread crumbs)**
**Vegetable oil for frying**

*Katsu Sauce:*
**⅓ cup catsup**
**¼ cup shoyu**
**¼ cup sugar**
**1½ teaspoons Worcestershire sauce**
**Dash of pepper**
**Dash of ground red pepper or hot sauce, optional**

Slice chicken breasts in half horizontally; pound gently to make ½-inch thick cutlets. Dip both sides of chicken into flour, beaten eggs, then dredge in panko. Fry cutlets in oil heated to 365 to 375°F, flipping when they are golden and crisp; drain on absorbent paper. Cut into 1-inch strips and serve with Katsu Sauce.

To prepare Katsu Sauce, combine all ingredients and mix well. Serve over fried cutlets.

# Tori No Mochiko Age
## Mochiko Fried Chicken

*Yield: 4 to 6 servings*

*The crispy, savory pieces of chicken are among Hawai'i's favorites.*

- 2 pounds boneless chicken thighs, quartered
- ¼ cup mochiko (rice flour)
- ¼ cup cornstarch
- ¼ cup sugar
- ½ teaspoon salt
- ¼ cup shoyu
- 1 clove garlic, finely minced
- ½ teaspoon grated ginger
- 2 eggs, lightly beaten
- 2 tablespoons minced green onion
- 1 quart vegetable or canola oil for deep frying
- 2 tablespoons toasted sesame seeds, optional

Combine and mix all ingredients thoroughly. Marinate for 2 to 3 hours or overnight. Deep-fry in oil heated to 350°F until done or golden brown. Drain on absorbent paper. Sprinkle with sesame seeds or serve with mustard/shoyu sauce, if desired.

# Teba No Togarashi Age
## Spicy Chicken Wings
*Yield: 8 to 10 servings*

T*hese wings are the perfect addition to any bento or appetizer tray.*

### *Spicy Sauce:*
- ½ **cup shoyu**
- 1 **tablespoon mirin**
- ½ **cup sugar**
- ½ **cup minced green onion**
- 1 **teaspoon Shichimi Togarashi**
  **(seven-pepper spice)**
- ¼ **teaspoon grated ginger**
- **Chili oil, optional**

- 5 **pounds chicken drumettes**
- 2 **cups flour**
- 1 **quart vegetable oil for deep frying**

Combine all ingredients for Spicy Sauce; mix well and set aside.

Dredge chicken in flour and deep-fry in oil heated to 350 to 375°F until golden brown, approximately 5 to 8 minutes. Drain on absorbent paper. While hot, dip cooked chicken in Spicy Sauce. Serve hot or cold as appetizer or side dish.

# Tori No Harusame Age
## Fried Chicken with Long Rice

*Yield: 4 to 6 servings*

The "pokey" surface of the fried chicken pieces from the deep-fried bean thread noodle coating will make this dish a conversation piece for your next party.

**1 pound boned chicken**
**2 tablespoons sugar**
**¼ cup shoyu**
**¼ teaspoon grated fresh ginger**
**1 clove garlic, crushed**
**½ cup cornstarch**
**2 eggs, slightly beaten**
**1 bundle long rice (bean thread)**
**1 quart vegetable oil for frying**

Cut chicken into bite-size pieces. Combine next 4 ingredients; marinate chicken pieces 1 hour; drain. Dredge in cornstarch, then dip in egg.

Soak long rice in warm water for 5 minutes; cut into 1-inch lengths. Coat chicken with long rice; deep-fry in oil heated to 365°F for 1 minute or until delicately brown. Drain on absorbent paper; serve hot with shoyu.

## *Hasu No Kimpira*
# Fried Lotus Root

*Yield: 4 to 6 servings*

**B**ecause of its unique, delicate flavor and crisp texture, lotus root makes a very unique stir-fried Japanese dish. Fresh lotus root is a beautiful vegetable because of the patterns formed by the hollow spaces that run the length of each root.

**2 medium sections lotus root**
**1 tablespoon oil**
**2 tablespoons shoyu**
**1 tablespoon sugar**
**1 tablespoon toasted sesame seeds**

Cut lotus root crosswise into ½-inch slices then into ½-inch strips. Sauté lotus root in oil for about 5 minutes. Add shoyu and sugar. Cook until sauce is absorbed. Add sesame seeds.

# Gobo No Kinpira
## Fried Burdock Root

*Yield: 6 to 8 servings*

**K**inpira is the most popular dish that features this brown burdock root, gobo. It was introduced to ancient Japan from China as an herbal medicine. Raw gobo is inedible and when cooked it is stringy, but it adds a unique texture and flavor to a dish. It is also used for tempura, simmered dishes, and soups.

1 tablespoon dried shrimp or ¼ pound pork, thinly sliced
1 tablespoon canola oil
1 pound gobo (burdock root), cleaned and slivered
3 tablespoons sugar
¼ cup shoyu
1 small red chili pepper, seeded and minced
Carrot slivers
Toasted sesame seeds

Sauté dried shrimp or pork in hot oil; add gobo and stir-fry 1 minute. Add remaining ingredients; continue cooking over medium heat until sauce is absorbed, approximately 1 to 2 minutes. Garnish with carrot slivers or sesame seeds, if desired.

## Variation:

**Sausage to Gobo Kinpira (Fried Sausage and Burdock Root):** Sauté ½ cup chopped Portuguese sausage with ½ pound juienned gobo 5 to 8 minutes in non-stick skillet over medium heat. Sprinkle 2 tablespoons sugar over; add ¼ cup shoyu and cook until shoyu is absorbed.

*Agemono*

# Onasu No Hasami-Age
## Stuffed Fried Eggplant

*Yield: 6 servings*

*S*tuffing the eggplant with a shrimp mixture, then crusting it with corn flakes before frying, adds a rich flavor to this otherwise bland vegetable.

½ **pound shrimps, finely chopped**
1 **tablespoon green onion, minced**
½ **teaspoon ginger juice**
1 **teaspoon salt**
1 **tablespoon flour**
6 **long eggplants or Lahaina eggplants**
2 **eggs, beaten**
1 **cup corn flake crumbs**
1 **quart vegetable oil**

### Sauce:
¼ **cup shoyu**
¼ **teaspoon ginger juice**

Combine first six ingredients and mix thoroughly. Cut lengthwise slit in eggplants. Stuff shrimp mixture into openings. Dip in egg and dredge in corn flake crumbs. Deep-fry in oil heated to 365°F for 2 to 3 minutes on each side or until golden brown. Serve hot with shoyu and ginger juice sauce.

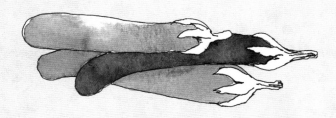

# Nasubi No Miso Kake
# Fried Eggplant with Miso Sauce

*Yield: 4 servings*

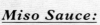

This is a tasty and simple way of preparing eggplant. The richness of the miso in the sauce compliments the delicate taste of eggplant. It is a great dish that can be eaten hot or at room temperature.

**2 round eggplants**
**1 egg, slightly beaten**
**2 tablespoons water**
**Flour**
**¼ cup vegetable oil**

*Miso Sauce:*
   **½ cup miso**
   **3 tablespoons sugar**
   **1 teaspoon shoyu**
   **1 tablespoon sake (rice wine)**
   **1 tablespoon Dashi (see options on pages 14-15)**
   **¼ teaspoon grated ginger**

Cut eggplant in half length-wise, then into ½-inch slices. Soak in water 10 minutes; drain. Combine egg and water. Dip eggplant into egg mixture then into flour. Fry in hot oil until both sides are crisp and brown.

Mix Miso Sauce ingredients together and cook over low heat until well blended. Serve hot over eggplant.

# Nabemono
## One-Pot Cooking

**N**abemono includes a variety of dishes prepared by simmering foods in a pot of savory broth. Sukiyaki and Shabu Shabu are two of the most well known. The beauty of a Nabemono dish is in the arrangement of the raw materials when presented to the guests for cooking. While nabemono dishes are delicious, part of their charm lies in the fact that guests cook and eat together at the table while socializing. Tasty morsels are taken from cooking pots and dipped into exotic sauces before being consumed.

# Sukiyaki
## Meat & Vegetables Cooked in Sauce

*Yield: 4 to 6 servings*

A Japanese food cookbook without a recipe for sukiyaki would be incomplete. There are hundreds of sukiyaki recipes and every family has its own. You, too, will develop your own in time.

Sukiyaki gained popularity after the Meiji period (1865-1912) when the Japanese began experimenting with foreign foods. There are numerous theories as to the origin of the name "sukiyaki." One theory is that because the Japanese did not want to use their kitchen utensils to cook this foreign dish, they used the blade of a plow (suki) as a grill for the meat instead, thus, sukiyaki—"broiled on the blade of a plow."

1¼ cups Sukiyaki Sauce (see page 143)
¼ cup beef or chicken broth
1 cup onion, sliced
1 pound beef, chicken, or pork thinly sliced
1 cup bamboo shoots, sliced★
½ block tofu, cubed
½ cup dried shiitake (mushroom), softened in water and sliced★
½ bunch long rice, softened and cut into 4-inch lengths★
2 cups watercress, cut into 1½-inch lengths
1 cup green onion, cut into 1½-inch lengths

Combine Sukiyaki Sauce and broth in skillet; arrange onion, beef, or chicken, bamboo shoots, tofu, mushrooms, and long rice attractively in sauce. Cook 3 to 4 minutes, spooning sauce over ingredients as they are cooking. Just before serving, add watercress and green onion. If desired, serve in individual dishes.

★1 can of Sukiyaki-No-Tomo may be used instead.

# Mom's Basic Sukiyaki Sauce

*Yield: 4½ cups*

This is a sweet shoyu sauce for cooking sukiyaki made of shoyu, sugar, sake or mirin, and dashi or broth. Other seasonings can be added, based on the cook's personal choices. For sukiyaki, thinly sliced beef is pan-fried, then some of this sauce is added along with vegetables.

- **2½ cups shoyu**
- **1½ cups sugar**
- **½ cup sake (rice wine) or mirin (sweet rice wine)**
- **½ cup Dashi (see options on pages 14–15) or water, optional**

Combine ingredients and mix well. Store in glass jar for use as base for Sukiyaki and other Japanese dishes.

# Shabu Shabu
## Shabu Shabu with Ponzu

*Yield: About 4 to 6 servings*

A great party dish that got its name from the sound made by swishing the ingredients back and forth in the boiling broth.

- 1½ pounds top sirloin, cut into paper-thin slices
- 1 (4-inch) piece dashi konbu
- 1 bunch watercress, cut into 1½-inch lengths
- 1 medium round onion, sliced
- 12 stems green onion, cut into 1½-inch lengths
- 1 box frozen broccoli spears, cut into 1½-inch lengths, optional
- ½ pound cooked udon (noodles)
- 6 cups chicken or beef broth or Dashi (see options on pages 14-15)

Ponzu Sauce (see page 149 or 72)
Sesame Seed Sauce (see page 148)
Momiji Oroshi (see page 93)

### Condiment:
Chopped green onion

Combine ingredients for Ponzu Sauce and pour into 4 small dishes and set before diners.

Arrange beef, vegetables, and noodles attractively on a platter and place on dining table. Bring broth to boil. Add konbu and remove after 1 minute. Dip beef in the boiling broth until it turns a light pink. Cook vegetables in the same manner. Add noodles last, cooking only until reheated. Each guest cooks a choice of meat or vegetables in the broth. Dip into Ponzu or Sesame Sauce with green onion to eat.

### Note:
The broth may be served as the last course, if desired. Any combination of your favorite vegetables may also be used for this dish.

# Teppan Yakiniku
## Grilled Beef

*Yield: 4 to 6 servings*

*T*his is another very popular dish, usually cooked and eaten around the table using a portable burner. This makes for a delightful dinner and the ingredients used are up to the cook. Dip cooked ingredients in choice of sauce.

    1½ **pounds rib-eye or top sirloin beef, thinly sliced**
    2 **small round onions, sliced**
    2 **bell peppers, seeded and sliced into rings**

*Marinade A:*
    2 **teaspoons toasted sesame seeds**
    1 **dried red pepper, seeded and minced**
    ¼ **cup minced green onion**
    1 **tablespoon red miso**
    1 **clove garlic, finely minced**

*Marinade B:*
    ¼ **cup sugar**
    2 **tablespoons mirin (sweet rice wine)**
    ¼ **cup shoyu**
    ¼ **teaspoon sesame seed oil**
    2 **tablespoons minced green onion**
    1 **clove garlic, crushed**
    ½ **-inch piece fresh ginger, crushed**

*Marinade C (Spicy):*
    ¼ **cup Korean hot sauce (Ko Choo Jung)**
    2 **teaspoons vinegar**
    2 **teaspoons shoyu**
    ½ **teaspoon sugar**
    1 **tablespoon toasted sesame seeds, crushed**
    2 **tablespoons minced green onion**

To prepare Marinade A, grind sesame seeds with pestle until oily; combine with other ingredients and mix well. To prepare Marinade B, combine ingredients and bring to a boil; cool. To prepare Marinade C, combine all ingredients and mix well. Set aside and use as marinade or dip.

Spoon marinade of choice over meat 4 to 5 minutes before cooking. Heat yakiniku grill or skillet; cook meat and vegetables over high heat until of desired doneness. Serve with remaining marinade as dip or prepare Teppan Yaki Sauce of choice on the next page. Serve with tossed green salad and dressing of your choice.

# Teppan Yaki Sauces

*Yield: 4 servings*

**S**auces are essentially a way of adding more flavor and sometimes an additional texture to any dish. They provide another layer, giving a dish extra depth—they are the finishing touches to any dish.

### Beef Sauce:
2 tablespoons Worcestershire sauce
½ cup catsup
2 teaspoons dry mustard
2 teaspoons lemon juice
1 tablespoon mirin (sweet rice wine)
2 tablespoons grated round onion

### Hot Sauce:
¼ cup rice vinegar
1 tablespoon mirin (sweet rice wine)
2 tablespoons shoyu
1½ tablespoons sugar
1 clove garlic, crushed, optional
2 tablespoons hot pepper sauce or dry mustard

### White Sauce (for vegetables):
3 tablespoons sugar
¼ cup rice vinegar
1 tablespoon mirin (sweet rice wine)
¼ cup grated daikon (Japanese radish)
½ teaspoon grated fresh ginger, optional
1 clove garlic, crushed, optional

### Sesame Seed Sauce:
½ cup white sesame seeds, toasted and ground
3 tablespoons Dashi (see options on pages 14-15)
2 tablespoons rice vinegar
1½ tablespoons shoyu
1 tablespoon mirin (sweet rice wine)

To prepare your desired dipping sauce, combine ingredients and mix thoroughly; serve in small individual dishes.

# Gyuniku No Bata Yaki
## Butter-Fried Beef
*Yield: 4 to 6 servings*

Slices of beef grilled in butter, accompanied by onions and green peppers, are served with ponzu sauce. For variety, add other vegetables of choice.

>   2 pounds beef, cut in paper-thin slices
>   1½ teaspoons salt
>   ¾ teaspoon pepper
>   2 medium round onions, quartered
>   2 green peppers, wedged
>   ¼ cup butter or margarine

>   *Ponzu Sauce:*
>   3 tablespoons shoyu
>   2 tablespoons rice vinegar or citrus juice
>   ⅛ teaspoon hot sauce, optional

Sprinkle beef slices with salt and pepper. Cook beef and vegetables at table in melted butter over medium heat.

Combine sauce ingredients; serve in individual dishes and use as dip for beef and vegetables.

## Variation:
Add vegetables of choice such as zucchini, bean sprouts, mushrooms, carrots, asparagus, okra, etc.

# Jingisukan–Nabe
## Genghis Khan Barbecue
### Yield: 4 servings

T he fascination with this dish is the special Genghis Khan pan with its dome-shaped cooking surface that allows fat to drain off. A cast-iron skillet may be used, however, the results will not be the same as the meat will cook in its fat.

- 1 pound beef (or lamb), cut into paper-thin slices, reserve fat trimmings
- 1 medium round onion, sliced
- 2 green bell peppers, wedged
- 1 small eggplant, sliced
- 4 dried shiitake (mushrooms), softened in water and drained

### Sauce:
- ¼ cup sake (rice wine) or mirin (sweet rice wine)
- ½ cup grated apple
- ½ cup shoyu
- 2 teaspoons sugar
- 1 clove garlic, pressed

### Condiments:
- ¼ cup minced green onion
- Minced lemon rind
- 2 tablespoons grated daikon (Japanese radish)
- Juice of one lemon
- Momiji Oroshi (see page 93)
- 1 small onion, grated
- 1 teaspoon grated fresh ginger

Arrange meat and vegetables attractively on individual platters. Food is cooked individually at the table using a Jingisukan (Genghis Khan) pan. Heat Jingisukan pan; place beef or lamb fat in the middle and have guests select and cook their choice of meat or vegetables. To prepare Sauce, bring sake to boil; add remaining ingredients and bring to a boil again. Dip in Sauce, with desired Condiments.

# Yosenabe
## Japanese Stew
*Yield: 4 servings*

This dish is the Japanese version of bouillabaisse, although, the ingredients are never allowed to cook for very long. This is a perfect table-top meal cooked in an earthenware pot, donabe, which holds and conducts heat evenly. Nabemono offers an informal and friendly way to share a hot meal. Of course, friendly conversation is a "must" with this kind of meal.

½ **pound ground pork, formed into meatballs**
**Flour**
**2 tablespoons oil**
**6 cups Dashi (see options on pages 14-15)**
½ **pound chicken, thinly sliced**
½ **pound shrimp, scallops, or clams, cleaned**
**1 cup bamboo shoots, sliced**
½ **pound fresh mushrooms, or 10 dried shiitake**
  **(mushrooms), softened in water**
**1 Chinese cabbage, or 1 pound spinach, cut in 1½-inch**
  **pieces**
**1 can (5-ounce) water chestnuts, sliced**
**4 hard-boiled eggs**
**2 tablespoons shoyu**
**1 teaspoon sugar**
½ **teaspoon salt**

Dredge pork meatballs in flour and pan-fry in hot oil until golden brown. Drain on absorbent paper and set aside.

Arrange each of the ingredients attractively on a separate dish or on a large platter. On dining table on portable burner, pour about 4 cups of dashi in skillet and bring to boil. Add chicken, seafood, vegetables, and eggs. Season with shoyu, sugar, and salt; cook 2 to 3 minutes or until of desired doneness. Add more broth and more seasoning as needed. Serve in individual dishes.

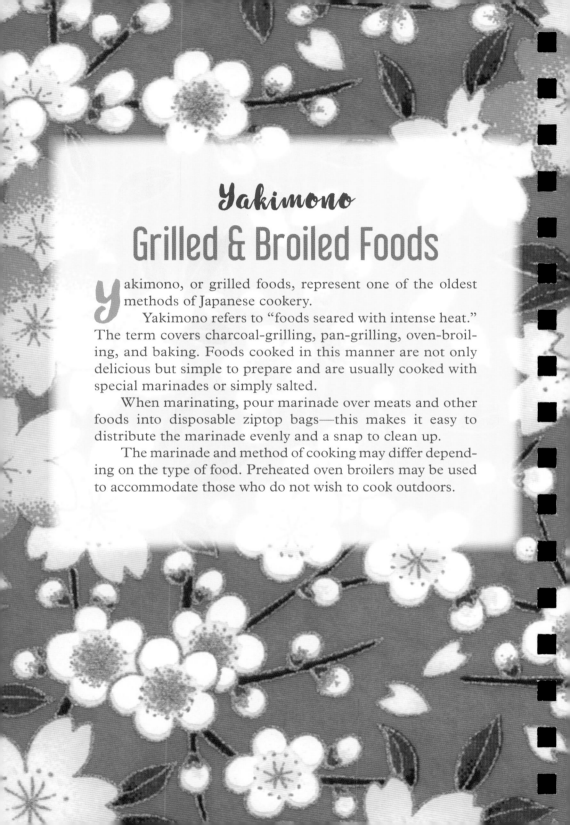

## *Yakimono*
# Grilled & Broiled Foods

**Y**akimono, or grilled foods, represent one of the oldest methods of Japanese cookery.

Yakimono refers to "foods seared with intense heat." The term covers charcoal-grilling, pan-grilling, oven-broiling, and baking. Foods cooked in this manner are not only delicious but simple to prepare and are usually cooked with special marinades or simply salted.

When marinating, pour marinade over meats and other foods into disposable ziptop bags—this makes it easy to distribute the marinade evenly and a snap to clean up.

The marinade and method of cooking may differ depending on the type of food. Preheated oven broilers may be used to accommodate those who do not wish to cook outdoors.

# Basic Teriyaki Sauces

*Yield: About 3 to 4 cups*

Scrumptious sauces, like Teriyaki Sauce, make any meal a success. *This sauce got its name from "teri" which means shine or luster and "yaki" which refers to the method of grilling or broiling.*

### Teriyaki Sauce #1:
    2 cups shoyu
    ½ cup sake (rice wine) or mirin (sweet rice wine)
    2 cups sugar
    1 clove garlic, crushed
    1½ teaspoons grated fresh ginger

### Teriyaki Sauce #2:
    2 cups shoyu
    ½ cup sake (rice wine) or mirin (sweet rice wine)
    1 cup brown sugar, packed
    1 clove garlic, crushed
    1 teaspoon grated fresh ginger

Combine ingredients in jar; cover and shake until well blended. Use as marinade for beef, pork, poultry, fish, shellfish, and lamb.

### Variation:

**Teriyaki Glaze:** Combine Teriyaki Sauce ingredients of choice in small saucepan, blend well and cook over low heat until thickened. Cool and use as glaze over cooked meats instead of marinating in Teriyaki Sauce, this produces a less salty end product.

# Matsu Kage Yaki
# Teriyaki Chicken

*Yield: 2 to 4 servings*

*C*hicken, marinated in teriyaki sauce and broiled on an outdoor grill was always a special treat. The kiawe charcoal truly enhanced the flavor of the succulent pieces of chicken.

**4 pieces boneless chicken breast★**
**¼ cup Basic Teriyaki Sauce (see page 153)**
**1 tablespoon toasted sesame seeds, optional**

Marinate chicken pieces in Teriyaki Sauce for 30 minutes. Broil on outdoor grill over low or medium heat, skin side up on grid. Baste frequently and turn; cook 10 to 15 minutes or until done.

★Whole broiler or frying chicken may be used. Cook over low or medium heat on outdoor grill for 40 to 60 minutes or until done. Wrap in foil, if desired.

## Variation:
**Namazu No Kabayaki (Broiled Teriyaki Catfish):** Substitute 1 pound catfish for chicken.

# Gyuniku No Teriyaki
## Teriyaki Beef
*Yield: 2 to 4 servings*

*B*eef teriyaki is a very popular Japanese dish which uses a sweet and shiny sauce for marinating as well as for glazing. Almost any meat can be prepared using this recipe.

**2 pounds beef slices or 1 piece steak, 1-inch thick**
**½ cup Basic Teriyaki Sauce (see page 153)**

Marinate beef in Teriyaki Sauce for half hour. Slash fat at 2-inch intervals for steaks. Broil on outdoor grill over high flame, basting frequently. Time: 8 to 12 minutes (rare), 12 to 20 minutes (medium), 20 to 30 minutes (well-done).

# Abarabone No Teriyaki
## Teriyaki Spareribs
*Yield: 4 to 6 servings*

*P*ork spareribs, teriyaki style, were always a special treat for me, as pork was not often served at our home. Whenever they were served, they were always lean, tasty, and tender.

**3 to 4 pounds spareribs**
**Water**
**1 cup Basic Teriyaki Sauce (see page 153)**

Simmer spareribs in water to cover for 20 to 30 minutes. Drain. Marinate in Teriyaki Sauce for 30 minutes or longer. Broil, basting frequently and turning occasionally, for 20 to 30 minutes or until done.

# Miso Yaki No Moto
## Basic Miso Sauces

*Yield: 4 to 6 servings*

**M**iso, a fermented soybean paste, is used in soups and sauces and also for pickling meat and fruit. Like so many other things in Japan, miso came from China via Korea in about the eighth century. As the Japanese didn't know much about fermentation back then, it was not food for the average person. It wasn't until the 1500s that miso began to be popular.

### *Miso Sauce Option 1:*
1½ cups miso
¾ cup sugar
1 to 2 tablespoons mirin (sweet rice wine)
½ teaspoon grated fresh ginger

1½ pounds fish fillet or top round steak, cut into serving pieces

### *Miso Sauce Option 2:*
¾ pounds sake kasu (rice wine dregs)
3 cups sugar
1 cup shoyu
1 cup sake (rice wine)
2 pounds red miso

5 to 6 pounds butterfish fillet steaks

Combine desired Miso Sauce ingredients. Marinate fish or beef slices in Miso Sauce Option 1 overnight. If whole fish is used, cut slashes on each side of fish and salt lightly. Stuff fish cavity with Miso Sauce. For butterfish fillet steaks, marinate in Miso Sauce Option 2 for 2 to 3 days.

Cook fish or beef slices on outdoor grill or in oven broiler over medium to high heat for 3 to 5 minutes on each side, or until of desired doneness. Whole fish may be fried or broiled.

# Tori To Onasu No Peanuts Yaki
# Chicken and Eggplant with Peanuts

*Yield: 6 to 8 servings*

*C*hicken and eggplants are marinated in a slightly sweetened shoyu-
peanut butter sauce to give them a unique flavor.

**2 long eggplants**
**½ teaspoon salt**
**8 boneless chicken thighs**

*Marinade:*
**6 tablespoons crunchy-style peanut**
 **butter**
**1 tablespoon lemon juice**
**1 tablespoon sake (rice wine) or**
 **mirin (sweet rice wine)**
**¼ cup sugar**
**¼ cup shoyu**
**1 small round onion, minced**

Slice eggplants diagonally into 1½-inch
slices. Soak in cold water for 30 minutes. Drain and sprinkle with salt. Cut slits
through chicken skin on both sides.

Combine Marinade ingredients and marinate chicken and eggplants
for 2 hours. Thread chicken and eggplant alternately on skewers.
Place on cold broiler pan; broil 25 to 30 minutes or until done.

# Gyuniku No Kushi Yaki
## Beef Kabobs

*Yield: 1 dozen kabobs*

Add some flair to your buffet with some colorful, tasty kabobs. Stick the skewers of cooked kabobs into a whole pineapple and place the arrangement on a bed of greens—absolutely awesome!

**½ pound top round steak**
**1 large green pepper**

*Marinade A:*
   **½ cup shoyu**
   **2 tablespoons sake (rice wine) or mirin (sweet rice wine)**
   **¼ cup sugar**
   **½ teaspoon grated fresh ginger**

*Marinade B:*
   **½ cup shoyu**
   **¼ cup mirin (sweet rice wine)**
   **¼ cup sake (rice wine)**
   **1 tablespoon miso**
   **¼ cup sugar**

   **Bamboo skewers**

Cut beef into ¾-inch cubes. Combine Marinade A ingredients and marinate beef 2 hours.

Seed green pepper; cut into 1-inch squares. Thread alternately with beef on skewers. Place on cold broiler pan; broil 4 to 5 minutes on each side or until of desired doneness. Baste occasionally while cooking.

## Variation:
**Butaniku No Kushi Yaki (Pork Kabobs):** Cut pork into bite-sized pieces and substitute for beef. Combine Marinade B ingredients and dip kabobs in marinade before grilling.

# *Yakitori*
# Chicken Kabobs

*Yield: 1 dozen kabobs*

**Y**akitori is one of Japan's favorite and famous dishes, easy to prepare, serve, and eat.

½ **pound boned chicken, cut in bite-size pieces**
2 **stalks green onion, cut in 1-inch lengths**
¼ **pound fresh mushrooms, cut in half**
**Bamboo skewers**

*Marinade Option 1:*
¼ **cup shoyu**
¼ **cup sake (rice wine) or mirin (sweet rice wine)**
2 **tablespoons sugar**
¼ **teaspoon sesame seed oil**

*Marinade Option 2:*
½ **cup shoyu**
¼ **cup mirin (sweet rice wine)**
¼ **cup sake (rice wine)**
1 **tablespoon miso**
¼ **cup sugar**

Thread green onion, chicken, and mushrooms on each skewer.

Combine desired Marinade ingredients; dip kabobs in marinade. Grill or broil 3 to 4 minutes or until done. Turn once or twice, brushing occasionally with Marinade, while cooking. Serve as side dish or appetizer.

# Mahimahi No Yakimono
## Broiled Mahimahi

*Yield: 4 servings*

Add a crispy crunch to one of Hawai'i's favorite fish fillets. The preparation is fast and easy—the flavor sooooo 'ono!

**1 pound mahimahi (or bass or butterfish) fillet**
**½ teaspoon salt**
**1 cup mayonnaise**
**1 cup corn flakes or bread crumbs**

Slice fish into ½-inch thick pieces to yield 4 to 6 serving pieces. Sprinkle with salt and coat with mayonnaise. Dredge fish in corn flakes or bread crumbs. Place on cold broiler pan. Broil 3 to 5 minutes on each side or until done.

# Sakana No Shio Yaki
## Salted Broiled Fish

*Yield: 2 to 4 servings*

Fish, lightly salted and broiled, was often enjoyed by my family. This is a very typical method of fish cookery in most Japanese kitchens as it is easy, fast, and delicious. Mom would always finish her broiled fish dishes with a generous dab of mayonnaise.

**1 whole fish (2 to 3 pounds); bream, 'ōpakapaka; scaled**
**and cleaned; allow about ½ pound per person**
**Salt to taste**
**Mayonnaise to taste, optional**
**Minced green onion, optional**

Scale and clean fish. Sprinkle lightly with salt; let stand 30 minutes. Rinse salt off and pat dry with paper towel. Gently prick sides with skewer. Lightly sprinkle again with salt until fish surface is completely salted. Cut slits into sides of fish; wrap tail in foil to prevent burning. Broil 5 to 9 minutes on each side, or until done. Spread mayonnaise over entire surface, if using. Broil additional 1 to 2 minutes or until mayonnaise bubbles. Garnish with green onions, if desired.

# Kani No Salada Yaki
## Hot Crab Salad

*Yield: 4 servings*

In the late 1940s, one of Dad's innovative specialties at his Paradise Garden Teahouse restaurant was his Ise Ebi no Salada Yaki. Today, this savory dish could be called the beginning of a local food trend, with the magic of mayonnaise.

**1 (6½-ounce) can crab, shredded**
**2 cups shredded cabbage**
**¼ cup finely chopped celery**
**¼ cup minced green onion**
**½ teaspoon salt**
**¾ cup mayonnaise, divided**
**Dash of pepper**

Combine all ingredients, except ½ cup mayonnaise. Toss gently and place salad in 4 individual baking shells. Top each with 2 table-spoons mayonnaise. Broil 1 minute or until mayonnaise bubbles. Garnish with paprika, if desired.

### Variation:
**Ise Ebi no Salada Yaki (Hot Lobster Salad):** Substitute 1 cup cooked lobster meat (cut into cubes) for crab.

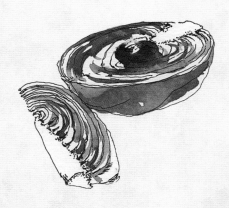

# Dashi Maki Tamago
## Seasoned Omelet Roll

*Yield: 4 to 6 servings*

Thin slices of this omelet roll can be tucked into a bento box as a sweet course. The technique is simple, though it may take some practice to make a perfect roll. Or, for a slightly different version, steam the egg mixture 5 to 6 minutes in a glass loaf pan, cut into desired sizes and serve as a side dish.

**¼ cup dashi or chicken broth**
**1 tablespoon mirin (sweet rice wine)**
**¼ teaspoon shoyu**
**¼ teaspoon salt**
**¼ teaspoon sugar**
**5 large eggs, beaten**
**Vegetable oil for frying**

### *Garnishes:*
**Parsley, beni shoga (red pickled
ginger)**

Combine dashi and seasonings; blend well and add to beaten eggs. Heat rectangular egg pan or skillet. Grease pan lightly and pour in one-third of the egg mixture. When egg is about 60 percent cooked, roll egg as you would a jelly roll toward the front of the pan using a wide spatula. When it is completely rolled, grease pan again, then push rolled egg to the back of the pan and grease front portion again.

Add another third of egg mixture. Lift rolled egg and allow egg mixture to flow under the cooked rolled egg. Repeat until all of the egg mixture is used. You may place fried egg roll on a "sudare" (bamboo mat) and roll into cylindrical shape. Let cool completely.

To serve, cut into about 1-inch thick slices. Garnish with parsley and pickled red ginger, if desired.

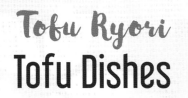

# *Tofu Ryori*
# Tofu Dishes

Soybeans play an important role in the Japanese diet. Among soybean products is a white, cheese-like product called tofu (soy bean curd) which is frequently served by the Japanese as it is rich in highly digestible protein.

Tofu is made from the milk of soybeans to which a coagulant is added, resulting in a custardlike curd that is tasteless but full of protein. The protein-rich milk is made by first wet-milling raw soybeans to produce a slurry called "go." This slurry is then boiled, pressed, and filtered through cloth to produce the "milk."

The two types of tofu that most are familiar with are:

- **Cotton tofu (momendofu):** the firmer tofu which is best for cooking. This tofu is preferred by tofu aficionados and referred to as more authentic.
- **Silken tofu (kinugoshi):** made from a richer milk, which is poured into a smooth-sided mold after the coagulant is added. The resulting tofu is soft, falls apart easily, and has a silky sooth texture from which it gets its name. This tofu is preferred for most tofu dishes and it's also good for dressings and dips.

# Hiya Yakko
# Chilled Tofu

*Yield: 4 servings*

A simple presentation of tofu that's well chilled shows off the quality of the ingredient. The flavor is pure and not masked by other ingredients or flavorings. You can have as many or as few condiments as you like.

> **1 block fresh tofu**
> **1 tablespoon minced green onion**
> **¼ cup katsuobushi (dried fish flakes)**
> **1 teaspoon grated fresh ginger**
> **3 tablespoons shoyu**

Cut tofu into 1-inch blocks. Keep refrigerated until ready to serve. To serve, place in bowl atop ice cubes; sprinkle with green onion and katsuobushi. Combine ginger and shoyu; use as a dip.

## Variation:

Serve with Ponzu Sauce (see page 72) served with grated daikon (Japanese white radish) and chili pepper as dip—simply delicious.

# *Yakidofu*
# Fried Tofu

*Yield: 4 servings*

"**W**hen in a bind regarding what to cook, just make tofu" is a saying commonly expressed in Japan. This goes to show how important tofu is as a protein source for the Japanese people. This is another favorite dish for many.

> **1 block tofu, quartered and drained**
> **½ cup flour**
> **½ cup vegetable oil for frying**
>
> *Ginger-Miso Sauce:*
> **¼ cup miso**
> **¼ cup rice vinegar**
> **1 teaspoon grated fresh ginger**
> **1 tablespoon sugar**
>
> *Ginger-Shoyu:*
> **¼ cup shoyu**
> **1 tablespoon grated fresh ginger**
> **2 tablespoons minced green onion**

Dredge tofu in flour. Fry in hot oil until light brown on each side. Drain on absorbent paper and serve with desired sauce.

To prepare sauces, combine ingredients and blend thoroughly.

## *Ebi Dofu*
# Shrimp Tofu

*Yield: 4 to 6 servings*

The Japanese are among the largest consumers of shellfish of all kinds and they are particularly fond of ebi (shrimp). Shrimp appear in soups, simmered dishes, salads, hot pots, tempura, broiled and steamed dishes—in other words, everywhere, in fresh and dried forms.

    ½ **pound shrimp, cleaned**
    **2 tablespoons vegetable oil**
    **1 medium round onion, sliced**
    **1 block tofu, cut into 1-inch cubes**

### *Seasonings:*
    **2 tablespoons sugar**
    **¼ cup shoyu**
    **¼ cup mirin (sweet rice wine)**
    **¼ teaspoon salt**

    **1 cup green onion, cut into 1-inch lengths**

Stir-fry shrimp in hot oil for 1 minute. Add onion, tofu, and Seasoning ingredients. Cook over medium heat for 3 to 4 minutes. Add green onion and cook additional minute. Serve immediately.

## *Variation:*
**Buta Dofu (Pork Tofu):** Substitute ½ pound pork, thinly sliced, for shrimp.

## *Kai Dofu*
# Clam Tofu

*Yield: 4 servings*

I n season, clams are sweet and juicy and give tofu a wonderful flavor.

- **1 onion, sliced**
- **1 tablespoon vegetable oil**
- **1 gobo (burdock root), slivered**
- **3 dried shiitake (mushrooms), soaked in 1 cup water and slivered**
- **⅓ cup shoyu**
- **3 tablespoons sugar**
- **1 tablespoon mirin (sweet rice wine)**
- **½ teaspoon salt**
- **1 block tofu, cut into 1-inch cubes**
- **1 (5-ounce) can boiled clams, reserve liquid**
- **4 stems watercress, cut into 1-inch lengths**
- **3 eggs, beaten**

Sauté onion in hot oil; add gobo and shiitake; cook 2 minutes. Add mushroom water, seasonings, and tofu; cook 10 minutes over low heat. Add remaining ingredients; cook 1 minute.

## Note:

Hokki-gai (Hokki-clams) may be substituted for canned boiled clams.

## *Shira Ae*
# Vegetables with Tofu Sauce
*Yield: 4 to 6 servings*

*A classic Japanese recipe uses tofu to make a creamy dressing for vegetables. The vegetables can be varied according to what is available but it is recommended that they be cooked separately. If desired, sesame seeds and shiitake mushrooms may be added for more depth and richness.*

> ½ **konnyaku (tuber root flour cake), slivered**
> 1 **cup slivered carrot**
> ½ **cup slivered takenoko (bamboo shoots)**
> 1 **bunch watercress, cooked and cut into 1½-inch lengths**

### *Stock:*
> ¾ **cup Dashi (see options on pages 14–15)**
> 2 **tablespoons shoyu**
> 1 **tablespoon sugar**
> ½ **teaspoon salt**

### *Tofu Sauce:*
> ½ **block tofu**
> 1 **tablespoon sesame seeds, toasted and ground**
> 2 **tablespoons sugar**
> ⅓ **cup miso**

Combine Stock ingredients; add konnyaku, carrot, and takenoko; cook for 5 to 6 minutes. Drain, cool, and set aside.

Prepare Tofu Sauce by squeezing excess water from tofu using double-thickness of cheesecloth. Mash with remaining sauce ingredients; mix well. Add watercress and cooled vegetables; mix thoroughly. Serve as a side dish.

# Swiss Chard Salad with Tofu Dressing

*Yield: 20 to 25 pūpū*

The first written record of tofu was sometime in 1183—nearly seven centuries after its arrival in Japan. However, that did not stop the Japanese from embracing tofu and refining it to suit Japan's subtle and delicate cuisine.

> **2 bunches Swiss chard (fudanso)**
> **8 cups water**

> *Tofu Dressing:*
> **1 block tofu**
> **½ cup miso**
> **3 tablespoons toasted white sesame seeds**
> **2 tablespoons sugar**
> **1 teaspoon dashi-no-moto, optional**

Break and separate fundaso stems from leafy sections. Bring water to a boil and cook stems for 5 minutes or until transparent. Add leafy sections; cook additional 3 to 4 minutes. When tender, drain in colander and rinse in cold water. Tear stems into ½-inch strips. Cut stems and leaves into 1-inch pieces; squeeze out excess liquid.

To prepare Tofu Dressing, wrap tofu in double-thickness of cheese-cloth and squeeze out excess liquid. Mix tofu, miso, sesame seeds, sugar, and dashi-no-moto thoroughly. Combine with greens; toss lightly and refrigerate 30 minutes or more before serving.

## Tofu No Hasami Age
# Fried Stuffed Tofu

*Yield: 4 to 6 servings*

Protein-rich tofu stuffed with raw fish cake is coated with bread crumbs, then fried in hot oil for a hearty side dish. Serve with shoyu, if desired.

½ **pound surimi (raw fishcake)**
¼ **cup minced green onion**
**Dash of pepper**
**Salt to taste**
**1 block tofu**
**1 egg, beaten**
**1 cup cracker or bread crumbs**
**2 cups canola oil for frying**

Combine first four ingredients and mix thoroughly. Cut tofu into 1 × 1½-inch blocks. Cut a slit in one side of each block and stuff with fishcake mixture. Steam 10 minutes; set aside to drain. Dip stuffed tofu in egg, dredge in crumbs, and pan-fry in hot oil for 1 to 2 minutes or until golden brown. Drain on absorbent paper and serve with shoyu.

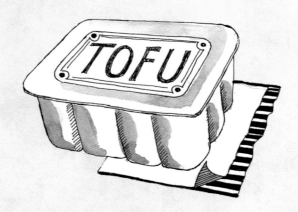

## *Tofu Tempura*
# Fried Tofu Fritters

*Yield: Approximately 2½ dozen*

Minced cooked shrimp and a variety of mixed vegetables are combined with tofu to make the Tofu Tempura mixture. The mixture is dropped into the hot oil to cook and served as an appetizer or side dish.

- **1 block tofu**
- **¼ cup cooked shrimp, chopped**
- **½ cup minced carrots**
- **⅓ cup green beans, chopped**
- **¼ cup finely chopped roasted peanuts**
- **⅓ cup gobo (burdock root), finely chopped**
- **2 tablespoons sugar**
- **1½ teaspoons salt**
- **3 eggs, beaten**
- **1 quart canola oil for frying**

Press out excess water from tofu using double-thickness of cheesecloth; strain through sieve or grind in suribachi. Add remaining ingredients and mix thoroughly. Drop by spoonfuls in oil heated to 365°F. Fry until golden brown. Drain on absorbent paper. Best served hot.

# *Tofu No Yakimono*
# Tofu Casserole

*Yield: 4 to 6 servings*

Aburage, fried bean curd pouches, are made with tofu that is cut into thin sheets and then pressed between bamboo mats and deep-fried twice. The result of a careful double frying procedure is crisp pouches that can be split open and stuffed or be used as an ingredient for casseroles and other Japanese dishes.

2 aburage (fried bean curd)
¼ cup shoyu
¼ cup water
1 tablespoon sugar
1 block tofu
¼ cup sesame seeds, toasted and crushed
½ cup carrots, slivered
⅓ cup slivered string beans
⅓ cup gobo (burdock root), minced
3 eggs, beaten
2 tablespoons sugar
1½ teaspoons salt
1 (10½-ounce) can cream of mushroom soup, optional

## Something About Tofu

Tofu is best when fresh, so plan to use it the day of purchase. To store with water, cover and refrigerate to prevent it from fermenting or breaking apart.

If tofu is to be kept more than a day, or not refrigerated, boil for 3 to 4 minutes before serving. To freeze, cut into cubes and store in airtight container. When frozen, it will turn yellowish brown and is then called koya-dofu. When ready to use, thaw, squeeze out excess water, and cook with shoyu and other seasonings, or add to sukiyaki.

Cook aburage in shoyu, water, and sugar for 5 minutes. Drain. Add tofu to sesame seeds, crush tofu. Slice aburage; add to tofu mixture with remaining ingredients. Mix thoroughly. Place in greased casserole dish, cover. Bake at 350°F for 30 minutes. Serve with heated cream of mushroom soup if desired.

# *Tofu No Teriyaki Dango*
# Teriyaki Tofu Burgers

*Yield: 4 servings*

O kara, a byproduct of the tofu-making process, is an inexpensive source of protein that can be used in many ways. When combined with ground beef it stretches the more pricey beef so more burgers can be made, but it also serves to lighten the burger mix.

- **1 pound ground beef**
- **1 egg**
- **¾ cup okara or kirazu (bean curd residue)**
- **2 tablespoons shoyu**
- **1½ teaspoons sugar**
- **¼ teaspoon salt**
- **¼ cup chopped onion**

### *Teriyaki Sauce:*
- **¼ cup shoyu**
- **1½ tablespoons sugar**
- **1 clove garlic, crushed**
- **1 teaspoon grated fresh ginger**

Combine first 7 ingredients; mix thoroughly and form into 8 patties. Combine Teriyaki Sauce ingredients and marinate burgers in sauce for 10 to 15 minutes. Place on cold broiler pan. Broil 4 inches from flame for 5 minutes on each side or to desired doneness. Baste occasionally.

## Unohana/Okara
# Seasoned Tofu Residue
*Yield: 6 cups*

Okara reminds the Japanese of the small white unohana flower. This dish's extravagantly poetic name disguise a very basic and inexpensive meal. Okara is virtually tasteless, but because it is light and spongy it absorbs flavors well.

### *Vegetables:*
½ cup carrot, slivered
1 konnyaku (tuber root flour cake), finely chopped
1 tablespoon dried shrimps, finely chopped
½ cup water
2 teaspoons salt

1 aburage, minced
½ cup dried shrimps, finely chopped
4 cups okara or kirazu (soybean curd residue)
½ cup vegetable oil

### *Seasonings:*
2 teaspoons salt
1 tablespoon sugar
1 tablespoon shoyu
¼ cup rice vinegar
1 cup minced green onion

Combine Vegetable ingredients; cook 5 minutes. Drain and cool.

Stir-fry shrimps and aburage in hot oil for 1 minute. Add okara and stir-fry constantly for 10 minutes or until okara is dry and flaky. Add Seasoning ingredients and stir until well-blended. Add cooked vegetables and green onion. Cook 1 minute.

## Aburage No Nitsuke
# Stuffed Fried Bean Curd in Shoyu

*Yield: 4 servings*

*A*burage (fried tofu) is unlike other tofu products. It can be opened up like a pouch and in this recipe it is cooked with a shoyu-based sauce and filled with a savory tofu-chicken mixture.

**4 aburage (fried bean curd)**
**3 cups boiling water**
**8 (6-inch) pieces kampyo (dried gourd)**

*Filling:*
**½ block tofu**
**½ pound boned chicken, slivered**
**2 tablespoons minced green onion**
**2 tablespoons finely chopped carrots**
**1 dried shiitake (mushroom), softened in water and minced**
**½ teaspoon salt**
**1 tablespoon sugar**

*Sauce:*
**2 tablespoons sugar**
**¼ cup shoyu**
**¼ cup sake (rice wine)**

Cut each aburage in half to make 2 smaller triangles. Carefully remove inner portion from each section. Pour boiling water over aburage; drain and squeeze out excess liquid.

Squeeze out water from tofu, combine with remaining Filling ingredients; mix well. Stuff aburage, up to ¼-inch from edge. Fold edges over and tie with kampyo. Combine Sauce ingredients and pour over stuffed aburage; simmer for 20 minutes.

# *Fukubukuro*
# Stuffed Tofu Pouches

*Yield: 16 pouches*

A simply delicious snack that can be made in minutes.

**8 small aburage
(fried bean curd)
8 pieces plain mochi (glutinous
rice cake)**

*Sauce:*
**1¼ cups chicken broth
2 tablespoons shoyu
1½ tablespoons sugar
1 tablespoon mirin
(sweet rice wine)**

Cut each aburage in half, then carefully pull apart to form pouches. Insert a piece of mochi into each pocket; secure with a wooden pick; set aside. Combine Sauce ingredients in saucepan; mix well and bring to a boil. Carefully place the pouches in the liquid—they should fit snugly upright against each other in the pot. Cover and simmer gently over low heat 25 to 30 minutes or until mochi softens. Remove wooden picks and serve hot, drizzled with a little sauce.

## *Agedashi Tofu*
# Deep-Fried Tofu in Broth

*Yield: 4 to 6 servings*

O ne Hundred Rare Tofu Recipes *was first published in 1782 in Osaka—a testament to the importance of tofu as a source of protein. One of the recipes featured was Agedashi Dofu, an all-time favorite.*

**1 block tofu (regular)**
**Flour for coating**
**1 quart vegetable oil for deep frying**

*Sauce:*
**1½ cups Dashi (see options on pages 14-15)**
**¼ cup mirin (sweet rice wine)**
**¼ cup shoyu**
**3 tablespoons cornstarch dissolved in 3 tablespoons water**
**1 tablespoon fresh ginger juice**

*Condiments:*
**½ cup fine bonito flakes**
**¼ cup minced green onion**
**1 tablespoon grated fresh ginger**

Cut tofu into eight square pieces; lay on clean cloth or absorbent towel; set aside to drain for 1 hour. Coat tofu with flour and deep-fry in oil heated to 335 to 350°F until light brown. Drain well on absorbent towel.

Combine Sauce ingredients and bring to a boil. Strain to clarify; return sauce to pan and heat again. When mixture begins to boil, thicken with cornstarch mixture; add ginger juice.

To serve, arrange fried tofu in serving bowls; add hot sauce. Top with bonito flakes, green onions, and grated ginger.

## *Variation:*
Grated daikon (white radish) may be added to sauce, if desired.

# *Okashi*
# Desserts & Confectionery

All types of sweets and cakes fall under the collective name okashi in Japan. Confectionery was introduced by the Chinese around the eighth century. Before that, fresh and dried fruits, honey, vegetables, nuts, and other naturally sweet foods had to satisfy the craving for sweets.

Traditionally, the Japanese seldom served desserts like Westerners. Instead, sweets made of glutinous rice, azuki beans, kanten, and sugar are served as snacks with tea or coffee. A traditional Japanese dessert uses no dairy products, although contemporary desserts do. A few favorite okashi recipes are featured in this section.

# *Kanten*

## Basic Kanten

*Yield: 32 (1 × 2-inch) pieces*

**A**gar agar (kanten) bar, a seaweed gelling agent, is used to prepare the congealed dishes.

**2 sticks white kanten**
**1 quart water**
**1 cup sugar**
**Few drops red or green food coloring**

Wash kanten, tear into small pieces, and soak in water for 30 minutes. Add sugar; cook until sugar and kanten dissolve, stirring occasionally. Add coloring; strain into 8-inch square pan. Cool and chill until it congeals. Cut into desired shapes.

## Dad's Cinnamon Kanten

*Yield: 32 (1 × 2-inch) pieces*

**A**ny special occasion or family gathering called for my Dad's special Cinnamon Kanten with spicy cinnamon candy from Holland included as a "secret" ingredient.

**3 sticks red kanten**
**5 cups water**
**¼ pound cinnamon ball candy**
**3 cups sugar**
**½ teaspoon vanilla extract**

Follow directions for Basic Kanten above.

*How to cut Kanten and Yokan:*

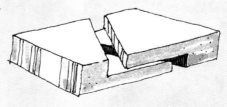

# Pineapple No Awa Yuki
## Foamy Pineapple Kanten

*Yield: About 8 to 12 servings*

The light and airy pineapple kanten bars made for a most attractive platter of "sweets" for any gathering.

**2 sticks white kanten**
**4 cups water**
**1 cup sugar**
**¼ teaspoon lemon extract**
**1 cup canned crushed pineapple, drained**
**Drop of yellow food coloring, optional**
**1 egg white**

Tear kanten into small pieces and soak in water for 30 minutes. Cook until kanten dissolves. Add all but 2 tablespoons sugar; stir until sugar dissolves. Add lemon extract, crushed pineapple, and food coloring.

Beat egg white until soft peaks form. Add remaining 2 tablespoons sugar; beat until stiff. Add kanten slowly and beat until well blended. Pour into 8-inch cake pan and chill until congealed. Cut into desired shapes or sizes.

# Jell-O Kanten

*Yield: 32 (1 × 2-inch) pieces*

*T*here were times in the 1940s when kanten was not available at the markets—Jell-O (gelatin) was the substitute.

**2 (3½-ounce) boxes flavored gelatin**
**1¼ cups sugar**
**2 cups boiling water**
**1½ cups cold water**
**¼ cup unflavored gelatin (4 envelopes)**
**1¼ cups cold water**
**1 teaspoon lemon extract, optional**

Combine flavored gelatin and sugar. Dissolve in boiling water. Add cold water and mix until well blended.

Sprinkle unflavored gelatin over cold water to soften. Add to hot flavored gelatin mixture. Add flavoring; mix thoroughly. Pour into 8-inch cake pan. Refrigerate until firm; cut into desired shapes.

## Koshi An
# Sweetened Bean Paste

*Yield: 5 to 5½ cups*

Although azuki bean paste can be purchased ready-made it is not too difficult to make yourself. If you do, you can adjust the level of sweetness to suit your palate. This bean paste is the basis of a number of Japanese sweets.

**2 pounds dried lima or azuki beans**
**5 cups sugar**
**1½ teaspoons salt**

Wash and soak beans in water overnight. Drain; cook in water to cover, adding more water as needed, until beans are very tender (1 to 1½ hours).

Grind beans in suribachi (mortar and pestle), then strain, using sieve. Discard outer skins. Using muslin bag, squeeze out excess water. Add sugar and salt to pulp; cook, stirring constantly, until thick enough to hold shape. Cool and use as filling for manju, mochi, ohagi, etc.

## Variation:
**Tsubushi An:** DO NOT STRAIN beans after grinding in suribachi.

## Kona Kohi–Azuki Kanten
## Kona Coffee-Red Bean Gelatin

*Yield: 12 to 16 pieces*

*I* magine a refreshing, chilled dessert with
the unique combination of flavors of Kona
coffee, sweetened milk, and azuki bean,
topped with a dollop of whipped cream and
ice cream … the perfect dessert for summer!

**¼ cup (4 envelopes) unflavored
gelatin**
**½ cup cold strong Kona coffee**
**2½ cups hot Kona coffee**
**1 (14-ounce) can sweetened
condensed milk**
**1 can prepared Tsubushi An
(coarsely mashed red bean
paste)**
**Dash of salt, optional**

Sprinkle gelatin over cold coffee; let stand 15 to 20 minutes. Combine hot coffee with condensed milk and Tsubushi An; mix well. Add softened gelatin to hot mixture and stir until gelatin dissolves. Pour into 8 × 8-inch pan and refrigerate until firm. Cut into desired sizes. If desired, garnish with dollop of sweetened whipped cream or vanilla ice cream.

## An Pan
# Bean Paste Rolls

*Yield: 2½ to 3 dozen*

A very popular roll filled with a dollop of sweetened azuki bean paste. It can be served with hot green tea or as a dessert after a meal.

**1 package activated dry yeast**
**¼ cup warm water**
**1 cup boiling water**
**3 tablespoons shortening**
**1 cup sugar**
**¾ teaspoon salt**
**2 eggs, beaten**
**4½ to 5 cups flour, sifted**
**1½ cans prepared An**

**Melted butter or 1 egg**
   **yolk beaten in**
   **1 tablespoon water**
**Toasted sesame seeds**

Soften yeast in warm water. Combine boiling water, shortening, sugar, and salt; cool to lukewarm. Add softened yeast. Add eggs; mix well. Add enough flour to make smooth, soft dough. Knead on lightly floured board. Place in greased bowl; turn once to grease surface. Cover and let rise until double in bulk (about 1 to 1½ hours). Punch down; shape into a smooth ball. Cover and let rest 10 minutes. Pinch off walnut-size pieces of dough and flatten to form circles. Fill with 1 tablespoon An and pinch edges together to seal. Place on greased cookie sheet; brush tops with melted butter or egg bath; sprinkle with sesame seeds. Let stand until double in bulk (about 45 minutes to 1 hour). Bake at 375°F for 15 minutes or until golden brown.

# Kasutera
## Castella Sponge Cake

*Yield: 6 to 9 servings*

This golden sponge cake was introduced to the Japanese by the Portuguese. The cake ages well, so, it can be baked 2 to 3 days before serving. Often small, dainty squares with hot green tea or as strawberry shortcake topped with sweetened whipped cream and berries.

**6 egg yolks**
**¾ cup sugar**
**2 tablespoons lemon juice**
**1 tablespoon lemon zest**
**1 teaspoon vanilla extract**
**¼ cup water**
**1 cup cake flour, sifted**
**6 egg whites**
**½ teaspoon cream of tartar**
**¼ teaspoon salt**

Beat egg yolks until thick and lemon-colored. Beat in sugar gradually, about 1 tablespoon at a time. Continue to beat until mixture is consistency of mayonnaise. Add lemon juice, lemon zest, and vanilla. Mix until thoroughly combined. Add water, 1 tablespoon at a time, mixing well after each addition. Fold in flour, 1 tablespoon at a time, until all of the flour has been added.

Beat egg whites until frothy. Add cream of tartar and salt, beating until stiff peaks form. Fold meringue into batter. Pour into ungreased 9-inch square cake pan. Bake at 325°F for 1 hour or until done. Invert and cool before serving.

## *Yokan*
# Dad's Bean Paste Dessert

*Yield: 32 (1 × 2-inch) pieces*

Yokan is a sweet jelly made with bean paste and sugar and set with agar agar, to be eaten with green tea. The slight bitterness of the green tea balances the sweetness of the yokan.

**2 sticks white kanten**
**1½ cups water**
**¼ pound butterscotch candy, optional**
**1 cup sugar**
**½ teaspoon salt**
**1½ cups prepared canned Koshi An**
**(sweet azuki bean paste)**

Tear kanten into 1-inch pieces and soak in water with butterscotch candy for 30 minutes, or until candy dissolves. Cook over medium heat until kanten dissolves, stirring constantly. Add sugar and salt; stir until dissolved. Add Koshi An and continue to cook over medium heat, stirring constantly, until mixture comes to a boil.

Pour into 8 × 8 × 2-inch pan and cool. Cut into desired shapes.

### Variations:
- **Macadamia Nut Yokan:** Add 1 cup finely chopped macadamia nuts to recipe.
- **Kuri (Chestnut) Yokan:** Add ¾ cup chopped cooked chestnuts to bean paste mixture.

## *Yaki Manju*
# Baked Bean Paste Pastry
*Yield: 2 dozen*

*I*f you enjoy baking anything fast, easy, and 'ono you will enjoy this recipe for manju. I especially like to use candied pineapple pieces or canned apples as fillings.

### Dough:
  2½ **cups flour**
  ½ **teaspoon salt**
  1 **tablespoon sugar**
  1 **cup vegetable oil**
  6 **tablespoons cold water**

  1 **cup prepared canned Koshi An (sweet azuki bean paste) or Tsubushi An (coarsely mashed red bean paste)**

Combine flour, salt, and sugar; blend thoroughly. Add oil and water to dry ingredients and mix thoroughly. Shape dough into small rounds, using approximately 1 tablespoon dough. Flatten dough to form circles. Place a generous teaspoonful of an in the center of each circle and pinch edges together to seal. Place seam side down on ungreased cookie sheet. Bake at 400°F for 30 to 35 minutes or until golden brown.

## Variations:
**Easy Yaki Manju:** Use two 10-ounce cans refrigerated buttermilk biscuits instead of mixing own dough. Fill centers of dough with cooked sweet potato, canned apple, peach, or candied pineapple pieces instead of an for filling.

## Mushi Manju
# Steamed Bean Cake

*Yield: 3 dozen*

Here's another recipe for a quick dessert. This makes a delicious snack with green tea or even a tasty omiyage for friends and family.

**3 cups flour**
**1 cup sugar**
**4½ teaspoons baking powder**
**¼ teaspoon salt**
**½ cup milk**
**¼ cup vegetable oil**
**3 egg whites**
**1½ cups prepared canned**
   **Tsubushi An (coarsely mashed red bean paste)**

Combine first four ingredients and mix thoroughly. Combine milk, oil, and egg whites; add to dry ingredients and mix well. Shape dough into small round balls, using approximately 1 tablespoon. Flatten dough to form circles. Place a teaspoonful of Tsubushi An in the center of each circle and pinch edges together to seal. Place in steamer lined with waxed paper. Steam 15 minutes.

# Sata An Da Gi
## Japanese Doughnuts

*Yield: 2½ to 3 dozen*

Hot and tasty fresh homemade doughnuts can be at your fingertips at a moment's notice.

- 3 cups flour
- 1 cup sugar
- 4½ teaspoons baking powder
- ½ teaspoon salt
- 3 eggs, slightly beaten
- ¼ teaspoon vanilla, optional
- 1 cup milk
- 1 quart vegetable oil for deep-frying

Sift dry ingredients together. Combine eggs, vanilla, and milk; beat well and add to dry ingredients. Mix thoroughly. Drop by teaspoonfuls into oil heated to 375°F. Cook about 2 minutes or until golden brown. Drain on paper towel, and roll in sugar, if desired.

# Chichi Dango
# Microwave Milk Dumplings

*Yield: About 36 pieces*

This has been one of my favorite snacks since small-kid time. It's now easier than ever to make it in the microwave oven. This is one of the first things my grandson learned to make.

**1 (10-ounce) package mochiko**
**1 (13.5-ounce) can coconut milk**
**¾ cup sugar**
**½ teaspoon vanilla extract**
**Few drops red or green food coloring**
**Cornstarch or katakuriko (potato starch)**

Grease 5-cup microwave tube pan. In a medium bowl, combine all ingredients except cornstarch; mix until smooth. Pour mixture into prepared pan; cover with plastic wrap.

Rotating pan several times during cooking, microwave at medium-high power for 10 minutes. Let stand a few minutes. Pull mochi from sides of pan and invert onto a board dusted with cornstarch or potato starch. Cool. Cut into ¼-inch pieces. Coat each piece with cornstarch or potato starch.

## Variation:
**Kinako Mochi (Soybean Powder Dumplings):** Dredge dumplings in kinako before serving or wrapping individually.

# An Mochi

*Yield: 2 to 2½ dozen*

*Japanese classic! If you love the texture and flavor of mochi, you will certainly enjoy this chewy mochi with a taste of azuki.*

**2⅔ cups water**
**1 cup sugar**
**3 cups mochiko (rice flour)**
**½ teaspoon salt**
**1 cup katakuriko (potato starch) or cornstarch**
**1½ cups canned or homemade Koshi An (sweet azuki bean paste) OR Tsubushi An (coarsely mashed red bean paste) (see page 186)**

Combine water and sugar; bring to a boil. Combine mochiko and salt; make a well in the center and add the hot sugar syrup, all at once. Mix until ingredients are well-blended. Knead dough on pastry cloth or board sprinkled with cornstarch or potato starch, 20 to 30 times, or until dough is smooth and elastic. Pinch off walnut-size pieces of dough; flatten to form circles. Fill center of each circle with a tablespoon of An and pinch edges together to seal. Serve with tea.

# *Dorayaki*
# Sweet Bean-Filled Pancakes

*Yield: 8 Dorayaki or 16 pancakes*

Sweet bean paste is traditionally sandwiched between two pancakes to resemble a little "gong," hence its name Dora (meaning gong) Yaki. For a smaller portion, the pancakes may be folded in half and the inside filled with a little of the bean paste.

  1 egg
  1¼ to 1½ cups milk
  1 tablespoon vegetable oil
  2 cups biscuit mix
  1½ cups prepared Koshi An (sweet azuki bean paste)
   (see page 186)

Combine egg, milk, and oil; mix until well-blended. Add all at once to biscuit mix, stirring until dry mixture is moistened. Pour batter on hot, lightly greased griddle. Turn when cakes bubble and brown second side.

Form Koshi An into walnut-size balls. Flatten and place between 2 pancakes.

# Ohagi
## Red Bean Paste Rice

*Yield: 8 to 10 pieces*

I was introduced to Ohagi as a teenager during a month's stay in Japan visiting my grandparents in Yamaguchi Ken. The glutinous ball of rice, covered with azuki bean paste, was served as a snack accompanied by a cup of fragrant green tea.

**1 cup mochi rice (glutinous rice)**
**1 cup rice**
**2¼ to 2½ cups water**
**1 can prepared Koshi An (sweet azuki bean paste) or Tsubushi An (coarsely mashed red bean paste)**
**¼ cup sugar**

Wash and drain rice. Add water; cover and let stand 1 hour. Bring water to a boil in covered pot; reduce heat and continue boiling until water level equals rice level, about 5 minutes. Reduce heat to low and cook additional 10 to 15 minutes or until done. Turn heat off; steam 10 minutes before shaping into 8 to 10 rice balls.

Combine An with sugar; cook over low heat for 5 minutes. Cool; encase rice balls with an using a piece of cheesecloth.

# Nomimono
# Beverages

*B*everages are called nomimono in Japanese, the most popular non-alcoholic of which is ocha (green tea). Sake (rice wine) is Japan's most well known alcoholic drink and the term is also used to refer to other alcoholic drinks.

## Ocha
## Tea

*Yield: 4 cups*

*T*ea is served throughout the day in Japan and it is inconceivable to have a Japanese meal without it, so here's how to make a cup of green tea.

**1 tablespoon green
   tea leaves
4 cups hot water**

Place leaves in tea bag or directly into heated clay or ceramic teapot. Pour hot water over tea leaves. Steep 1 or 2 minutes before serving.

### Notes:

The color aroma and shape of the leaves define their quality. Japanese green tea should not be brewed with boiling-hot water. The better the quality of tea, the lower the water temperature should be.

## Popular types of Japanese tea

**Ban-cha:** This is an everyday drinking tea frequently served at restaurants. The color of the tea is yellowish-green and many varying qualities are available.

**Genmai-cha:** Green tea is blened with kernels of toasted and popped brown rice. Many families favor this tea with its rich and nutty flavor.

**Gyokuro:** Its name means "jewel dew" and it is the highest quality tea made from young tender leaves picked in early spring. The tea is highly fragrant and sipped on its own or accompanied with wagashi (Japanese sweets), but not served with a meal.

**Hoji-cha:** This roasted bancha tea has a nutty, woody flavor. It is most often served with a meal, especially breakfast. This tea may also be served cold.

**Ko-cha:** Black tea is usually served with milk/cream and sugar.

**Kobu-cha:** Made from seasoned kelp.

**Mat-cha:** Made from the finest quality of tea, it is in a class of its own with its bright green color. The powdered tea is used in the Japanese tea ceremony.

**Mugi-cha:** Made from roasted whole grains of barley and technically not a tea. However, it is often sold in tea bags that are infused in cold water, then served chilled during summer.

**Sen-cha:** A green tea made of very tender leaves that comes in many gradations of quality. The tea's delicate flavor is a blend of subtle sweetness and bitterness. It is one of the more popular green teas.

## Processing tea leaves

Top-quality tea such as mat-cha gyokuro and sen-cha are protected from direct sunlight for one to three weeks before being harvested in early May, increasing the level of amino acid in the young leaves and reducing bitterness. The freshly picked leaves are then immediately steamed to prevent fermentation and discoloration. They are then dried by a rolling and scrunching process, then by hot air.

# Sake
# Rice Wine

## Classic Japanese Toast of "Kampai!"

Sake is a clear, fine, colorless wine with a fragrant aroma and subtle flavor. It was first brewed thousands of years ago as a sacred offering to the gods and is still used to toast marriages, births, and other special occasions.

The Japanese have been drinking sake since ancient times and it has played a vital role in the development of Japanese cuisine. Though the consumption of European-style wine has increased more than tenfold in Japan and is more common with everyday meals, sake remains the favorite alcoholic drink for meals like kaiseki (formal banquet). As such, it is developing into more of a connoisseur's drink.

More than 6,000 brands of sake are produced in Japan, with each brand producing a few different types, leading to a staggering 55,000 different kinds of sake sold in Japan. Jizake, regional sake, is seeing a rise in popularity over inferior mass-produced types. Some of the favorite alcoholic drinks of Japan include:

**Ama-zake:** A glutinous rice gruel combined with rice koji (a culture of mold grown on steamed rice). It is a mild, sweet drink especially enjoyed warm on a cold night.

**Otoso sake:** A sweet rice wine spiced with medicinal herbs. It is a tradition in Japanese families to take a sip of otoso to begin an auspicious New Year of extended life free of problems.

**Sake (rice wine):** The most popular brew of Japan was recorded as early as 712 in the Kojiki (record of ancient matters). It is a light, white rice wine made by using top-quality newly harvested rice.

**Sho-chu:** A popular drink among young Japanese adults. It is a colorless, distilled drink made either from high-energy grains and products such as buckwheat, millet, barley, sesame seeds, corn, carrots, rice, and sweet potatoes or molasses. There are two classifications of sho-chu, depending on the method of distillation—koh sho-chu or otsu sho-chu.

**Ume-shu (plum wine):** A delightful drink served chilled during the summer or at room temperature at other times.

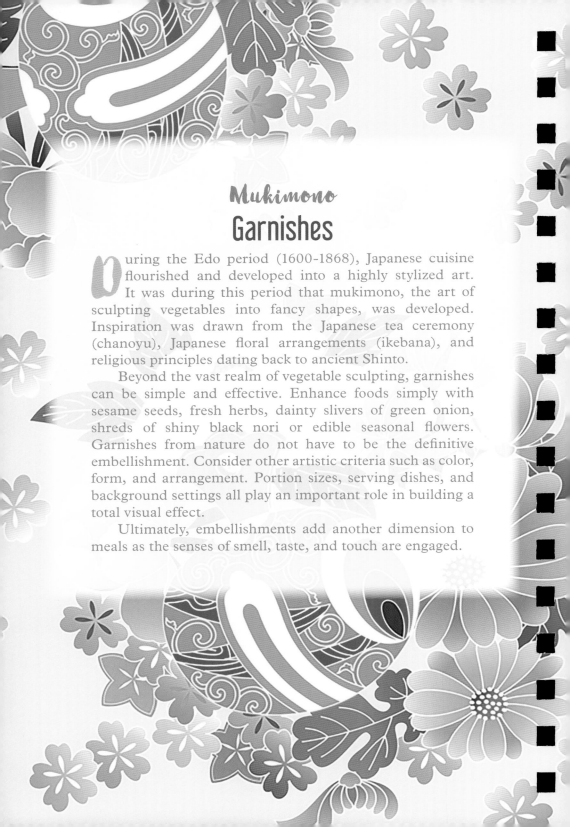

## Mukimono
# Garnishes

During the Edo period (1600-1868), Japanese cuisine flourished and developed into a highly stylized art. It was during this period that mukimono, the art of sculpting vegetables into fancy shapes, was developed. Inspiration was drawn from the Japanese tea ceremony (chanoyu), Japanese floral arrangements (ikebana), and religious principles dating back to ancient Shinto.

Beyond the vast realm of vegetable sculpting, garnishes can be simple and effective. Enhance foods simply with sesame seeds, fresh herbs, dainty slivers of green onion, shreds of shiny black nori or edible seasonal flowers. Garnishes from nature do not have to be the definitive embellishment. Consider other artistic criteria such as color, form, and arrangement. Portion sizes, serving dishes, and background settings all play an important role in building a total visual effect.

Ultimately, embellishments add another dimension to meals as the senses of smell, taste, and touch are engaged.

*learned vegetable sculpting from my dad during the time he owned and operated Paradise Garden, a Japanese-style teahouse in the Liliha district.*

## Useful Garnishing Tools

Cookie cutters

Canape cutters

Metal flower-shaped cutters

Radish-rosette cutter

Citrus zester

Citrus scorer

Straight paring knife

Curved paring knife

8- to 10-inch chef's knife

Crinkle-edged vegetable cutting knife

Vegetable peeler

Melon baller

Benriner cutter

Kitchen scissors

Assorted molds and cups for shaping rice

Wooden picks

Bamboo skewers

Paper towels

Food coloring kit

Zip-top plastic bags

## Stork

Select long daikon (white radish) with a slight curve. Cut daikon into shape of stork. With a sharp knife, carve in shape of thigh, neck, head, wings, and tail. Use bamboo skewers or wooden chopsticks for legs, cloves for eyes. Use one-half of a large potato for stand.

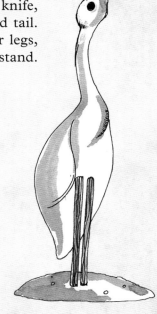

## Turtle

Cut pineapple skin into shape of turtle. Cut daikon (white radish) into shape of legs and head. Use the tip of a pineapple leaf for the tail. Use cloves for eyes.

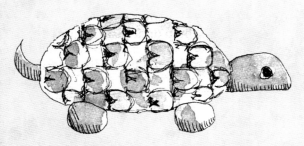

## Fish Net

The most challenging mukimono was the edible "fish net" which, for presentation of a fish dish, would be cast over a spectacular whole red fish in a boat-shaped black lacquer dish, as if it had just been caught.

Select daikon (Japanese white radish) that is of even cylindrical shape. Pierce center of daikon with ice pick; remove and push chopstick through center.

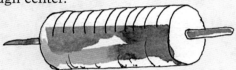

Starting at one end, make a straight row of 1-inch slits, ⅛-inch apart, inserting knife until it touches the chopstick. Make the second row of slits between those in the first row, overlapping the slit length half-way as shown.

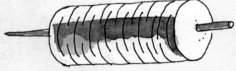

Make the third row of slits in line with the first, and the fourth row in line with the second. Repeat until the last row overlaps and fits between the first row of slits.

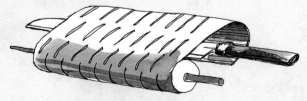

Sprinkle daikon lightly with salt; let stand a few minutes. The net is now ready to be cut. Use a very sharp, thin-blade knife, slicing very thinly and in one continuous piece. Salt occasionally while slicing to prevent daikon net from breaking. Re-roll onto chopstick until ready for use.

## Daikon (White Radish) Camellia

Cut 1 medium daikon into 3 sections; pare.

Round off both ends and one side as shown by dotted lines. Taper center so that it is about ½-inch narrower than ends.

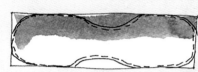

Cut very thin slices from end to end forming a petal. Repeat until 5 or 6 petals are cut for each flower.

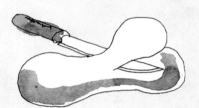

Pierce skewer through ½-inch square daikon for reinforcement. Assemble petals, laying largest one on bottom, criss-crossing one on top the other to form camellia.

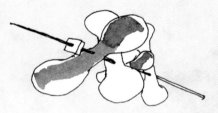

Cover skewer tip with rosette made by cutting thin V-shaped slashes around a ¾-inch piece of daikon. Tint if desired.

Place completed flower in ice water to crisp. Arrange with mock orange leaves or other greenery, using one-half of a potato or daikon as base.

## Peonies

Cut extra large daikon (white radish) into 3 sections of different lengths (6-, 4-, and 2-inch sections). Pare daikon and round off sections as for camellia, leaving center about ½-inch narrower than ends.

Score or cut 2 notches on both sides of daikon as shown, leaving top center slightly pointed.

Cut very thin slices from end to end, forming a petal. Repeat until 5 petals are cut for each flower. Use each daikon section to make one flower.

Pierce skewer through ½-inch square daikon for reinforcement. Assemble petals, laying largest one on bottom, criss-crossing one on top the other to form peony.

Cover skewer top with rosette made by cutting thin V-shaped slashes around a ¾-inch piece of daikon. Place in ice water to crisp. Tint before arranging on daikon or potato stand with hibiscus or mock orange branches.

*Mukimono*

# Traditions and Celebrations

Japan's many traditional festivities are times of both reverence and revelry, some honoring ancestors, others celebrating the joys of the present. Most are rooted in the dominant religions—Buddhism and Shintoism.

Rituals performed at Japanese festivals are generally significant rites of passage in an individual's life, meant to summon good spirits and ward off bad luck. Celebratory foods are key to all of these events.

Japanese families in Hawai'i have maintained many of these celebrations and their traditions of deliciousness.

## New Year's Day

Shogatsu or oshogatsu, the new year's celebration, is a time of clean starts, clean houses, and clean souls. The rest of Asia may celebrate the Lunar New Year, but the first of January is Japan's big bash. Many businesses shut down for three days, temple visits are required of the Shinto faithful, and families gather for the sharing of osechi ryori, or new year's foods.

Filled with ritual and symbolism, shogatsu is the most important holiday and a key part of the culture in Japan and in the Japanese-American community in Hawai'i.

The elaborate celebration starts the night before, on the eve, when soba is eaten for good luck, the long buckwheat noodles symbolizing longevity.

The next day a tiny cup of otoso—warm sake—comes before another kind of soup: ozoni. A myriad regional recipes exist for this special mochi soup, but they all have one thing in common, the mochi. Ozoni represents strength and prosperity.

Osechi ryori are traditional delicacies filled with symbolism, generally arranged in a four-tiered jubako (lacquered box):

- Kazunoko (herring roe): fertility
- Kuromame (black beans): good health and success
- Konbumaki (seaweed stuffed with chicken or pork): happiness
- Kinton (mashed sweet potato with chestnuts): yellow color is believed to bring good fortune
- Kamaboko (fishcake): red and white colors are a lucky combination, bringing happiness
- Hasu (lotus root): symbolizes the wheel of life
- Tai (bream or red snapper): good health

Not every Japanese family in Hawai'i observes New Year's with all these foods, and many supplement with local and American favorites. Our family's party also included baked ham, macaroni or potato salad, roasted chicken, fried noodles, kalbi, and more.

## Omiyage

For thousands of years, omiyage, the giving of gifts, has been an important part of the Japanese culture. It initially began as a means of gaining the goodwill of those in power and the rituals that surrounded early gift-giving were extraordinarily complex.

Many cultures have a gift-giving tradition, but the Japanese elevate this to an art, or perhaps an obsession. Shops dedicated to omiyage shopping are found throughout Japan, selling gift boxes of food items with each morsel inside wrapped to make sharing easy.

The practice has been adopted to a milder extent in Hawa'i. We carry manju, mochi, sweet bread, chips, cookies, and dim sum back and forth to the neighbor islands, or bring beef jerky or any specialty item from places we visit. We even give "te omiyage" (small gifts) when visiting friends and family. I was taught to never go "empty-handed" when visiting anyone.

A handmade gift, given from the heart, is the most cherished of all. The joy of a gift is in the making as well as in the giving. Some gifts from your kitchen created with love and aloha could be yaki manju, castera, yokan, chichi dango (see Okashi section, pg 182) and more.

To the Japanese, a gift is an exterior sign of inner feelings. Think of omiyage as an expression of gratitude, a mark of friendship, and a sign of respect. The custom of gift-giving has been adopted by many in Hawai'i, where generosity, thoughtfulness and sharing are characteristic of island living.

## Boy's Day

The symbol of Boy's Day is the carp, a fish known to live long and prosper, swimming against currents and able to jump up waterfalls. Its strength is celebrated on the fifth day of the fifth month as families wish for lives of courage for their boys.

Carp-shaped windsocks are flown, one for each son in the household, and samurai dolls are put on display.

Boy's Day treats include mochi of many kinds, but specifically kashiwa mochi (wrapped in an oak leaf) and kushi dango (multicolored mochi balls on sticks).

May 5 is also celebrated as Children's Day, an official holiday in Japan honoring boys and girls.

*Japanese carp, called koi, hung on display for Boy's Day.*

*My grandchildren Stephen and Alissa.*

## Girl's Day

Hinamatsuri, a festival of dolls, is celebrated on the third day of the third month and is marked by displays of imperial court dolls in Heian-era costumes, arranged in tiers from the emperor and empress down through the royal attendants.

The date of March 3 places Girl's Day at the beginning of spring, when peach trees are in bloom—this is reflected in the party foods of the occasion. Hishi-mochi is a

*My granddaughter, Alissa.*

diamond-shaped layered rice cake colored pink for peach flowers, white for snow, and green for spring's budding growth. Chirashizushi, sushi rice with toppings in springtime colors, is also traditional. Sweets tend toward a peachy pink and comprise mochi of many kinds.

By the way, those dolls may be put out sometime in February, but must be put away on March 4—failure to do so is said to harm a daughter's chances of marriage.

*Dolls on display for Girl's Day.*

## Yakudoshi

Think of yakudoshi celebrations as doses of prevention. They are traditionally held in birthday years believed to be bad luck—yaku meaning "calamity"; doshi meaning "year." Prayer and parties are viewed as ways to ward off bad luck, thus minimizing potential damage.

The ill-omened ages are 24, 41, and 60 for men; 18, 32, and 36 for women. (Note that these are the years as marked outside Japan. Within Japan, because a person's birth year is counted as year 1, yakudoshi years are marked a year later). It is thought to be good luck for the celebrant to wear red for health and long life.

In later years certain birthdays are also marked as special, without the baggage of bad luck. For men, the 60th, known as kanreki, is a nod to the traditional Chinese calendar with its 60-year cycles. It acknowledges a man's completion of one life cycle.

*Dad's beiju celebration for his 88th birthday.*

Men and women both may celebrate ga no iwai, or further rites of passage, in particular 77 (kiju), 88 (beiju) and 99 (hakuju). Beiju is also known as yone no iwai, or rice celebration, because the kanji for 88 resemble those for "rice." The special designation recognizes the essence of rice in Japanese culture.

## Obon

The summer festival honoring ancestors who've passed beyond is firmly rooted in Japan's Buddhist religion, a time to tend to gravesites and express gratitude for the debt owed to predecessors. The practice came to Hawai'i with Japanese laborers on the plantations.

Obon has evolved locally to reach far beyond the core religion, shared by celebrants of all backgrounds. Festivals are held throughout the summer, marked by nights of dancing around a tower where taiko drummers keep the beat for hours.

*Dancers at a typical Hawai'i bon dance.* (Honolulu Star-Advertiser)

Festival foods are part of the draw: teriyaki, yakisoba, grilled mochi, oden, andagi, sushi of many varieties, and much more. They are typically sold along with hot dogs, hamburgers, and grilled corn on the cob. Also, shave ice, because dancing can be a sweaty business.

## Cha No Yu (The Way of Tea)

Cha no yu is a Japanese ceremony consisting of the serving and taking of tea in accordance with an elaborate ritual. The ceremony—which involves the preparation and presentation of matcha, or powdered green tea—is more than a social occasion. It serves to create an island of serenity, to refresh the senses, and to nourish the soul.

Brick-shaped loaves of tea were introduced into Japan from China in the eighth century. Matcha was brought to Japan in the twelfth century by Zen monks returning from China. Originally, tea was consumed for its medicinal properties and also used as a stimulant to stay awake during all night meditation. Tea drinking eventually spread to the nobility, who freely dispensed it during social gatherings.

The aristocracy in Japan cultivated an austere and aesthetic custom of drinking tea which permeated the life of the samurai and the religious world. It continues today, centuries later, as Cha no yu, a unique synthesis of philosophical, cultural, and religious beliefs and traditions. Cha no yu has been influenced by Shintoism, Chinese Taoism, and Zen Buddhism. It focuses on four virtues: Harmony (wa), Respect (kei), Purity (sei) and Tranquility (jaku).

## Kaiseki Ryori

The Japanese cuisine that was sired by Cha no yu is Kaiseki Ryori. Originally a simple meal consisting of rice, soup, fish, and perhaps a vegetable and garnish, it has evolved into an elaborate meal that epitomizes Japanese cuisine.

A typical Kaiseki Ryori meal includes food from each of the categories of food listed in this cookbook. The food that is served with the tea is very special. To plan the menu, to select an array of ingredients and serving dishes, to arrange food with creative artistry, and to serve in "Kaiseki Style" is indeed a most gratifying experience!

# The Japanese Pantry

## Basic Principles of Japanese Cooking

- **Ingredients must be fresh and of top quality.** Cooking time is short and basic shopping know-how is a primary skill one must learn in order to recognize freshness and quality in fruits, vegetables, and meats.
- **All ingredients are chopped, diced, sliced, or cut into interesting bite-size pieces.** More emphasis and time are spent on this aspect of food preparation than on the actual cooking of the food. A very decorative effect is attained by cutting the ingredients in a variety of shapes and sizes.
- **The presentation of the food is designed to be beautiful.** Garnishes are kept at a minimum and the food is simply and neatly arranged on beautiful plates or platters of various shapes. The simplicity of the arrangement of neatly cut cooked food and a fresh vegetable garnish emphasizes the natural beauty of the food.
- **Japanese flavorings and spices are important flavor highlights.** Of various seasonings used, miso, shoyu, sugar, and vinegar are most important. Sake (rice wine), mirin (sweet rice wine), and dashi (soup stock) are also used to flavor many dishes.

# Decorative Ways of Cutting and Slicing

*apanese food preparation is a fine art form, with the cutting of vegetables playing a key role. Depending upon the dish and the cooking method, a cook selects the most appropriate way to cut the ingredients to achieve an attractive visual presentation and ease of eating with chopsticks. Some examples:*

**Hangetsu-giri:** To cut into half-moon shapes.

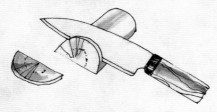

**Hyoshigi-giri:** To cut into rectangular shapes.

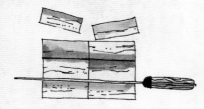

**Icho-giri:** To cut into pie shapes.

**Katsura-muki:** To cut into 2-inch lengths, thinly slice while turning. The vegetable will curl naturally, resembling a flat sheet when straightened. Recommended for daikon (white radish), carrot, and cucumber.

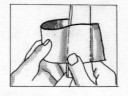

**Koguchi-giri:** To cut into small, round uniform slices.

**Mentori:** To cut round vegetables into quarters (pie shapes), slicing off sharp edges.

**Mijin-giri:** To mince.

**Ran-giri:** Cut long, thin vegetables like carrots and burdock diagonally, turning while cutting into oblique pieces.

**Sainome-giri:** To cut into small cubes; to dice.

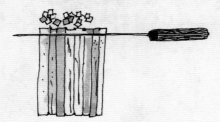

**Sasakaki-giri:** To sliver or shave, cut vegetables such as carrots and burdock root as you would sharpen a pencil.

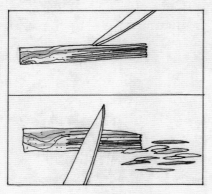

**Sen-giri:** To cut into thin strips or slivers; used in cutting daikon, carrot, burdock root.

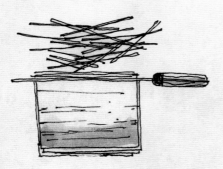

**Shinobi-hocho or kakushi-hocho:** To cut slits in vegetables where they are not seen; this is done to hasten the cooking process.

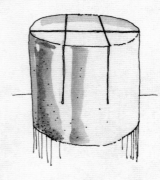

**Tanzaku-giri:** To cut into rectangular shapes; then into long, thin slices.

**Wa-giri:** To cut into round, uniform slices.

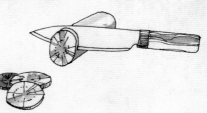

# Japanese Cooking Utensils

**Chuka nabe:** The Japanese term for the Chinese wok. It is used for stir-frying, steaming, and deep-frying.

**Genghis Khan griddle:** A special, dome-shaped griddle or skillet with grooves that allow the juices of foods being cooked to drip down and collect around the edge of the dome.

**Donabe:** An earthenware casserole dish with a lid, used to cook foods directly over heat.

**Hashi:** Chopsticks; assorted lengths are available. Both bamboo and metal ones are used for cooking. Ivory and lacquer ones are used for eating.

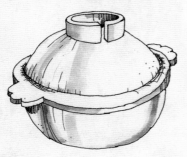

**Knives:** Japanese knives are designed for a variety of purposes. The knives are sharp and heavy. To use, keep the point stationary, raise the back, and let the weight of the knife do the cutting.

**Yoto:** Similar to a French knife, used for all-purpose cutting and slicing.

**Deba-bocho:** For heavy chopping and cutting

**Sashimi-bocho:** A long, slender knife used for slicing raw fish and soft ingredients into thin pieces.

**Oshiwaku:** Wooden mold for making oshizushi (pressed or molded sushi).

**Shabu shabu nabe:** The Japanese term for the Chinese "hot pot." Used for cooking at the table.

**Shamoji:** Rice paddle made of varnished wood or bamboo.

**Sudare:** Bamboo mat used for making maki-sushi, and rolling omelets and vegetables.

**Sukiyaki nabe:** A round, flat-bottomed cast-iron pan used for preparing sukiyaki. Coat with oil before storing to prevent rusting.

**Suribachi and surikogi:** Japanese version of the mortar and pestle. It is made of earthenware and the inner portion of the bowl is grooved or serrated, which aids in grinding or pulverizing.

**Tamago-yaki nabe:** Rectangular frying pan used for frying omelets, which are often rolled like a jelly roll, and egg sheets for sushi.

**Tempura nabe:** A round, flat-bottomed pan used to fry tempura.

**Teppan:** A flat, rectangular iron plate placed directly over the heat for table cooking.

**Zaru:** A bamboo basket used for draining and/or straining foods. It is the Japanese counterpart to a colander.

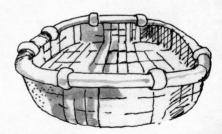

# Japanese Ingredients

**Bamboo shoot (takenoko):** Fresh young shoots of bamboo, used in many ways.

**Bok choy (chingensai or shakushina):** A leafy green vegetable popular in Chinese cooking.

**Burdock (gobo):** Root vegetable usually stir-fried and seasoned with soy sauce; also pickled.

**Chestnuts (kuri):** Sweet cooked chesnuts are made into a paste and used in confections.

**Chinese cabbage (hakusai):** Vegetable often added to one-pot dishes; also popular in pickles.

**Eggplant (nasu or nasubi):** Served grilled, fried, steamed and deep-fried.

**Ginger (shoga):** Used in Japanese cooking in many ways, puts zest in any dish or drink.

**Japanese mustard greens (mizuna):** Japanese cabbage commonly used in salads and soups, especially at New Year's.

**Gourd strips (kanpyo):** Made from the the dried flesh of the yugoo, gourd.

**Lotus root (renkon):** The rhizome of the water plant. Suitable for a wide variety of recipes; popular for its crunchiness and shape.

**Japanese cucumbers (kyuri):** These have fewer seeds and are less watery than the common cucumber.

**Mugwort (yomogi):** A wild grass or herb used to flavor buckwheat noodles and mochi.

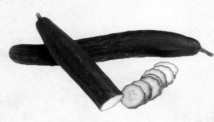

## Mushrooms

**Shiitake:** Most popular mushroom to flavor Japanese dishes.

**Enoki:** Thin and stringy white mushrooms sold in bunches; good in soups or one-pot dishes.

**Perilla or beefsteak plant (shiso):** The green leafed shiso is eaten fresh with sashimi; the dark purple variety is used primarily for pickling.

There are two types of shiso (beefsteak plant) available in the islands—green and red. The green leaves are normally used for dishes such as sashimi, tempura and vinegared salads. The red shiso leaves are used for pickling. The berries, stems and flowers of both types are used to garnish sashimi, soup and sauces.

**Pumpkin (kabocha):** Delicious steamed, baked, broiled, deep fried, and even puréed and used in dessert.

**Radish (daikon):** Japanese daikon is generally longer and thinner than the Chinese; good for grating and pickling.

### Seaweeds

Developing a taste for seaweed and learning to use it is well worth the effort. It is considered a health food and it certainly makes delicious stocks and sauces.

The three most commonly consumed varieties in Japan are nori, wakame, and konbu.

**Nori:** Sold in greenish-black sheets, nori is probably the most popular type of seaweed. Sushi rice and other ingredients are often rolled in this to make nori-maki sushi, and of course there's Spam® musubi, which is held together by half a sheet of nori.

**Wakame:** A long, curly seaweed added to soups and salad-like dishes like namasu. Fresh wakame is available in Japan and dehydrate; packaged versions are readily available in Hawai'i.

**Konbu:** Dried kelp, sold in many varieties. The long pieces of dried seaweed are washed, soaked in water to soften, then used to make dashi, a stock that is the basis of Japanese cuisine.

# Basic Japanese Sauces for Flavoring

## Shoyu

Shoyu is undoubtedly the single most important ingredient in Japanese cooking and is used in almost every recipe. It is often served as a dip on its own for sashimi, pickles, sushi, and many other dishes.

The ancient seasoning of Japan was called hishio and consisted of a preserve of what was at that time very scarce and precious: salt fermented with animal or vegetable protein and fiber. Grain hishio, fermented with grains such as rice, wheat and beans, was developed into miso and it exuded liquid that became shoyu. Using new techniques introduced from China, Japan developed its own type of soy sauce, shoyu, made from soy beans, wheat and salt. Japanese shoyu is quite different in aroma and flavor from the Chinese varieties.

## Miso

Miso's origin can be traced to the ancient seasoning called hishio. It was already being made in the 12th century and it is one of the oldest traditional Japanese ingredients.

Numerous kinds and brands of miso are available in supermarkets outside of Japan today. They are categorized into three basic grades according to strength of flavor and color: shiro miso (white—made with rice), aka miso (red—made with barley), and kuro miso (black—made with soy beans). It is used for simmered dishes, dipping sauces, and as a marinade for meat and fish.

## Su (rice vinegar)

Unlike shoyu and miso, rice vinegar, made from rice, has a delicate taste and is good for adding subtle flavors to Japanese cooking. Japanese rice vinegar has a mild, sweet aroma and is not as sharp as ordinary wine vinegar.

Vinegar has many qualities. It can be used to refresh and soften saltiness, acts as an antiseptic, and is a coagulant for proteins. It is useful from the preparation of ingredients to the final seasoning. Because the slightly mild, subtle, acidic flavor of Japanese vinegar disappears quickly, it should be added to hot dishes at the last minute.

## Mirin (sweetened rice wine)

This amber colored, heavily sweetened sake is used only in cooking. It is one of Japan's ancient seasonings.

Mirin has a faint sake aroma and syrupy texture, which adds a mild sweetness to the food. It is used for simmered dishes and in glazing sauces (such as tare for grilled dishes).

# Appendix

Glossary
Recipe Index
Ingredient Index
Other Books by the Author
About the Author

# Glossary

**Aburage:** fried bean curd

**Aemono:** dressed or mixed foods

**Agemono:** fried foods

**'Ahi:** Hawaiian name for yellowfin tuna

**Ajinomoto:** brand name for monosodium glutamate

**Ajitsuke nori:** seasoned dried laver; seaweed

**Aka miso:** fermented red bean paste

**Akule:** big-eyed scad

**An:** sweetened red bean paste

**An pan:** red bean paste-filled pastry

**Anago:** sea or conger eel

**Andagi:** Okinawan doughnut

**Araimo:** dasheen potatoes

**Awabi:** abalone

**Awase zu:** seasoned vinegar

**Ayu:** small river trout

**Azuki:** small red beans

**Beni shoga:** pickled red ginger

**Butaniku:** pork

**Castella:** sponge cake

**Chikuwa:** fish cake roll

**Chirimen iriko:** small dried sardines

**Daikon:** white Japanese radish

**Dango:** dumpling, meatball, or croquette

**Dashi:** basic broth; basis of all Japanese soups; used in cooking numerous dishes

**Dashi-no-moto:** Japanese instant soup stock granules

**Dashi konbu:** kelp used for soup stock

**Donabe:** earthenware casserole

**Ebi:** shrimp, prawn

**Edamame:** soybeans

**Endo mame:** peas

**Enoki:** thin and stringy white mushrooms

**Fu:** gluten cake

**Fudanso:** Swiss chard

**Funyu:** fermented bean cake

**Furikake nori:** Japanese seasoned seaweed mix

**Ginnan:** ginkgo nuts

**Ginshi yaki:** to cook in aluminum foil

**Gobo:** burdock root

**Gohan:** cooked rice

**Goma:** sesame seeds

**Goma-abura:** sesame seed oil

**Gu:** ingredients

**Gyoza:** Japanese dumpling

**Hakusai:** Chinese cabbage

**Hamaguri:** clams

**Hanagatsuo:** dried bonito shavings

**Hanagiri daikon:** thinly sliced dried white radish

**Harusame:** Chinese long rice; alimentary paste; bean thread

**Hashi:** chopsticks

**Hasu:** lotus root

**Hibachi:** charcoal braiser

**Hijiki:** type of seaweed

**Hiki niku:** ground beef

**Hiyamugi:** thin, chilled Japanese noodles

**Hokkigai:** large clams

**Hondashi:** fish-flavored soup stock granules

**Horenso:** Japanese name for spinach

**Ika:** squid, cuttlefish

**'Inamona:** roasted kukui nut, pounded and salted

**Inari sushi:** sushi rice stuffed in a cone-shaped fired tofu

**Iriko:** small, dried fish

**Ise ebi:** lobster

**Jagaimo:** potato

**Kabocha:** pumpkin, squash

**Kaibashira:** scallops

**Kaki:** oyster

**Kaki mochi:** Japanese rice crackers

**Kamaboko:** steamed fish cake

**Kampyo, kanpyo:** dried gourd

**Kanten:** agar agar

**Karashi:** dry mustard

**Katakuriko:** potato starch

**Katsuobushi:** dried bonito (tuna) flakes

**Kazunoko:** fish roe

**Kikurage:** fungus

**Kimisu:** salad dressing made with egg yolks and vinegar

**Kinako:** soybean flour

**Kinpira/kimpira:** burdock seasoned with sugar and soy sauce

**Kiri konbu:** julienne seaweed

**Kirazu:** soybean curd residue

**Kisu:** smelts

**Koimo:** Japanese taro; dasheen

**Koji:** rice lees

**Kome:** raw rice

**Konbu:** dried seaweed; kelp

**Konnyaku:** square cake made from tuber root flour

**Koromo:** batter

**Koshi an:** strained red bean paste

**Koya dofu:** dried bean curd

**Kūmū:** Hawaiian term for goatfish

**Kuri:** chestnut

**Kuro mame:** black beans

**Kushi-age:** fried kabobs

**Maguro:** Japanese name for tuna

**Mahimahi:** Hawaiian name for dolphinfish

**Makina:** celery cabbage; won bok

**Manju:** bean paste-filled bun

**Matcha:** powdered green tea

**Matsutake:** mushroos grown in pine forests

**Menrui:** noodles

**Mikan:** Mandarin oranges

**Mirin:** sweet Japanese rice wine

**Miso:** fermented Japanese soybean paste

**Miso zuke:** marinated in soybean paste

**Mitsuba:** Trefoil

**Mizuna:** Japanese cabbage

**Mochi:** glutinous rice cake

**Mochi gome:** glutinous rice

**Mochiko:** rice flour

**Moi:** Hawaiian name for small threadfin fish

**Momiji oroshi:** grated white radish with red chili pepper

**Moyashi:** bean sprouts

**Mushimono:** steamed foods

**Nabemono:** one-pot dishes

**Naganegi:** shallots

**Namasu:** vinegar-flavored Japanese vegetable dish

**Nameko:** tiny wild musthrooms with slippery coating

**Nasu/nasubi:** eggplant

**Negi:** green onion; leek

**Nerigarashi:** mustard paste

**Nibosi:** small dried fish

**Nimono:** foods cooked in seasoned liquid

**Niku (gyuniku):** beef

**Nin niku:** garlic

**Nira:** chives

**Nishime:** cooked vegetable dish; Japanese "stew"

**Nishime konbu:** Japanese kelp; tangle

**Nitsuke:** simmered in soy sauce and sugar

**Nori:** dried laver; seaweed

**Nuka:** rice bran

**Oboro:** dried shredded shrimps

**Ocha:** green tea

**Ogo:** Japanese term for seaweed

**Okara:** soybean curd residue

**Omochi:** rice cake

**Onaga:** Japanese term for red snapper

**'Ōpakapaka:** pink snapper

**Panko:** Japanese style bread crumbs

**Piman:** bell pepper

**Ponzu:** mixture of soy sauce and citrus juice

**Rakkyo (rankyo):** pickled scallion

**Ramen:** saimin; noodles

**Renkon:** lotus root

**Saba:** mackeral

**Sakana:** fish

**Sakazuke:** sake cup

**Sake:** Japanese rice wine

**Sake kasu:** rice wine residue

**Sanbai zuke:** vegetables pickled in vinegar, soy sauce, and sugar

**Sansho:** Japanese pepper

**Sashimi:** raw fish

**Sato imo:** Dasheen taro

**Satsuma imo:** sweet potato

**Sawara:** fish from the mackeral family

**Senbei:** Japanese wafers

**Sengiri daikon:** dehydrated radish strips

**Seri:** watercress

**Shibi:** yellow fin tuna; maguro

**Shichimi togarashi:** seven flavors spice; blend of pepper leaf, poppy seed, rape seed, hemp seed, dried tangerine peel, and sesame seed

**Shiitake:** dried mushrooms

**Shiozuke:** pickled in salt

**Shira ae:** food combined with mashed tofu sauce

**Shirataki:** stringy konnyaku; thread-like noodles made from arrowroot flour

**Shiro miso:** white soybean paste

**Shiso:** beefsteak plant

**Shoga:** fresh ginger

**Shojin ryori:** Buddhist vegetarian cooking

**Shoyu:** Japanese term for soy sauce; seasoning made from roasted corn and steamed soybeans mixed with malt-mold, salt, and water, then fermented.

**Shungiku:** spinach like vegetable; of the chrysanthemum family; chrysanthemum leaf

**Soba:** buckwheat noodles

**Somen:** fine noodles made from wheat flour

**Su:** rice vinegar

**Sudare:** bamboo mat

**Suimono:** clear soup

**Sumiso:** vinegar-miso sauce

**Sunomono:** vinegared foods; salads

**Suribachi:** serrated bowl used for grinding; mortar and pestle

**Sushi:** vinegar-flavored rice

**Sushi meshi:** prepared sushi rice

**Suzuke:** vegetables pickled in vinegar

**Tai:** bream

**Takenoko:** bamboo shoot

**Tako:** octopus

**Takuwan:** pickled white radish

**Tamago:** egg

**Tamagoyaki:** fried egg sheet

**Tama negi:** round onion

**Tara:** cod

**Tare:** dipping sauce

**Tempura:** fritters

**Teriyaki:** soy-flavored sauce; grilling food while basting with teriyaki sauce

**Tofu:** soybean curd or cake

**Togan:** squash; Chinese winter melon

**Togarashi:** red chili pepper

**Tori niku:** chicken

**Tosa zu:** seasoned vinegar sauce

**Tsubushi an:** coarsely mashed red bean paste

**Tsukemono:** pickled vegetables

**Udon:** thick noodles made of wheat flour

**Ulua:** Hawaiian name for trevally/ crevalle

**Umani:** vegetable-meat dish

**Umeboshi:** red pickled plum

**Unagi:** eel

**Uni:** sea urchin

**Ushiojiru:** clear fish/shellfish soup

**Wakame:** lobe leaf; dried seaweed

**Warabi:** fiddlehead fern shoots

**Wasabi:** green horseradish powder

**Wari bashi:** wood chopsticks

**Weke:** Hawaiian term for spot fish

**Yaki dofu:** tofu which has been fried and slightly hardened

**Yaki manju:** baked pastry with red bean filling

**Yakimono:** grilled foods

**Yaki niku:** Japanese term for grilled meat

**Yakitori:** Japanese-style grilled or broiled chicken

**Yatsumi zuke:** relish dish

**Yokan:** sweet red bean paste confection

**Yuba:** dried bean curd

**Yuzu:** citrus fruit similar to lime

**Zaru:** bamboo colander

# Recipe Index

# Ingredient Index

# Other Books by the Author

## As Author

Cook Japanese Hawaiian Style (Listed as Best-Seller), 1974

Hawaiian Pūpū Party Planner, 1974

Hawaiian Potpourri, 1975

Maxi Meals for Mini Money, 1975

Cook Japanese Hawaiian Style Volume II, 1976

New World of Cooking with Muriel, 1979

Cooking with Hari and Muriel, 1994

From Hawai'i's Kitchen: Homemade Gifts of Sweets & Treats, 2005*

Holiday Gift Giving Recipes, 2005*

Little Hawaiian Holiday Gift-Giving Recipes, 2005*

Hawai'i's Party Food, 2007*

Japanese Cooking Hawai'i Style, 2006*

Little Hawaiian Party Food Cookbook, 2007*

Little Hawaiian Cookbooks: Tastes & Flavors of Pineapple, 2007*

What Hawai'i Likes to Eat, 2007*

Hawai'i Cooks with Spam®, 2008*

Hawai'i Cooks & Saves, 2008*

What Hawai'i Likes to Eat, Hana Hou, 2009*

Little Hawaiian Condiments Cookbook, 2011*

Little Hawaiian Japanese Cooking Hawai'i Style, 2011*

Celebrating in Hawai'i: Favorite Recipes for Holidays and Special Occasions, 2016*

Favorite Recipes from the What Hawai'i Likes to Eat Series, 2016*

## As Editor/Chair

Heritage of Hawai'i: Cookbook vol. I (Gasco), 1965

Heritage of Hawai'i: Cookbook vol. II (Gasco), 1970

The Legacy of the Japanese in Hawai'i: Cuisine (JCCH), 1989

Tastes & Tales of Mōili'ili (Mōili'ili Community Center), 1997*

A Tradition of Aloha Cookbook (Japanese Women's Society), 1998

Flavors of Aloha (Japanese Women's Society), 2001

Hawai'i Cooks: A Korean Kitchen, 2013*

Hawai'i Cooks: An Okinawan Kitchen, 2014*

Hawai'i Cooks: A Portuguese Kitchen, 2014*

Hawai'i Cooks: A Chinese Kitchen, 2015*

Hawai'i Cooks: A Filipino Kitchen, 2016*

*Published by Muutal Publishing

240

# About the Author

**M**uriel Miura may be most recognized for her nationally televised cooking shows from the 1970s, *Cook Japanese Hawaiian Style* and *The New World of Cooking with Muriel*. While comfortable with all types of ethnic cuisine, Muriel's specialty has always been Japanese cooking where she adds a personal touch of Hawai'i to her foods. Muriel has written more than twenty cookbooks including *Cookies from Hawai'i's Kitchen, Hawai'i Cooks with Spam, Hawai'i Cooks and Saves, Celebrating in Hawai'i,* and *What Hawai'i Likes to Eat.* She also serves as co-editor of the "Hawai'i Cooks" series that includes *A Korean Kitchen, A Portuguese Kitchen, An Okinawan Kitchen, A Chinese Kitchen, and A Filipino Kitchen.*

Muriel graduated from the University of Hawai'i's Home Economics program and earned her graduate degrees in Home Economics Education from the University of Hawai'i at Mānoa and Columbia University of New York City.

Throughout her culinary career, she has judged food contests, taught community cooking classes and high school home economics, written articles about cuisine and food, and traveled to the New York World's Fair as a featured presenter and she won a prestigious award for outstanding demonstration. Muriel has also guest-starred on the popular *Hari's Kitchen* TV cooking show.

A Honolulu-born kama'āina, Muriel lives in Honolulu with her husband Yoshi and spends part of the year with her daughter Shari and her family on the mainland. Since her retirement from The Gas Company in 1993, she has been involved with a number of community service projects and she presently serves on the Board of Directors and Board of Trustees of the Mō'ili'ili Community Center.

# Other Titles in the Series

6 x 9 in. • Hardcover, wire-o binding

*A Korean Kitchen* explores a popular cuisine that relies on many vegetables, grains, fermented foods, and simple cooking techniques that require little fat. Meats are served as a small part of this vegetable-centric cuisine that focuses on many tasty side dishes on the table. Food writer Joan Namkoong draws on her island heritage to explain the Korean kitchen in Hawai'i, distinctly different from a Korean kitchen in Korea. (180 pp.)

*A Portuguese Kitchen* shares traditional recipes done Hawai'i-style by Wanda A. Adams. Portuguese cooking is at its heart very, very simple. The cuisine relies on the freshest, most carefully selected ingredients. It is comforting, but not edgy, earthy, sumptuous, and tasty. Find recipes for traditional Bacalhau (salt cod), Portuguese soup, Linguica Pica (spicy Portuguese sausage), Arroz Verde (Green Rice), Milho Frito (Fried Cornmeal Porridge), and more. (192 pp.)

*An Okinawan Kitchen* by Chef Grant Sato features the vibrancy of Okinawan cuisine—with all the heartiness of pork cooked many ways, the brightness of bitter melon and eggplant, and the purity of tofu prepared from scratch. This book is for those with Okinawan roots who seek to finally master classic rafute (braised pork) and goya champuru (bitter melon stir-fry) and for the adventurous cook willing to discover new takes on Okinawan flavors. (164 pp.)

*A Chinese Kitchen* provides insights into Chinese food traditions, culture, and experience in Hawai'i. Lynette Lo Tom captures the delicious cooking of her mother, extended family, and friends. There is a wide range of dishes including Winter Melon Soup, Chinatown-style Crispy Skin Roast Pork, and Mongolian Beef. Most of the recipes are Cantonese, as three-quarters of the Chinese workers who came to Hawai'i to work on the plantations were from Zhongshan (formerly called Canton). (216 pp.)

*A Filipino Kitchen* shows the diverse richness of colors, tastes, and flavors that define Filipino cooking and reflects Chef Adam Tabura's favorite childhood meals. Many of Adam's island-style recipes show new twists on traditional dishes. Plantation-style dishes are given a Filipino touch and Filipino dishes are given a tropical flavor. These recipes will appeal to those familiar with Filipino food and serve as a great introduction for those who want to learn more. (184 pp.)

*To order these titles and more, visit*
**www.mutualpublishing.com**